MALTESE

SMART OWNER'S GUIDE®

By Amy Fernandez

FROM THE EDITORS OF DOGFANCY MAGAZINE

CONTENTS

Maltese, a Smart Owner's Guide®
part of the Kennel Club Books® Interactive Series®
ISBN: 978-1593787-50-9. ©2011

Kennel Club Books Inc., 40 Broad St., Freehold, NJ 07728. Printed in China.
All rights reserved. No part of this book may be reproduced in any form,
by Photostat, scanner, microfilm, xerography or any other means, or incorporated
into any information retrieval system, electronic or mechanical,
without the written permission of the copyright owner.

*photographers include Isabelle Francias/BowTie Inc.; Tara Darling/BowTie Inc.;
Gina Cioli and Pamela Hunnicutt/BowTie Inc.; Shutterstock.com*

For CIP information, see page 176.

K9 EXPERT

If you have brought a Maltese into your home from a responsible breeder or a rescue group — or if you are planning to do so — congratulations! You have fallen in love with one of the most appealing breeds in all of dogdom. The Maltese is affectionate and energetic despite his small size, and the breed has been adored by many admirers throughout history.

The small, white fluffy dogs known collectively as bichons have been popular in the Mediterranean region for thousands of years. Those that lived on the island of Malta, off the southern coast of Italy, were known as Maltese. The breed was once called "Ye Ancient Dogge of Malta," a testament to his reign of more than 28 centuries as a canine aristocrat.

While the Phoenicians made Malta their home in about 1500 B.C., the island was populated by other Mediterranean peoples as far back as 3500 B.C. Malta was famed for its opulence, appreciation of the arts and high level of civilization. Here, the tiny Maltese thrived.

No owner was more devoted to his Maltese than Publius, the Roman governor of Malta. In the first century AD, the poet Martial wrote of this royal creature that "Issa is more frolicsome than Catulla's sparrow ... purer than a dove's kiss ... gentler than a maiden ... [and] more precious than Indian gems." Publius had a portrait commissioned so he could treasure her likeness forever.

A host of other classical poets, writers and philosophers have also praised the beauty,

intelligence and sweetness of the Maltese. The Greeks built tombs in tribute to their Maltese. Greek ceramic art depicting the dogs dates back to the fifth century. Queens reportedly served their Maltese the finest food out of gold vases. A model of a Maltese was even unearthed in Egypt.

The first Maltese exhibited in the United States was listed as a Maltese Lion Dog at the inaugural Westminster Kennel Club dog show in New York City in 1877.

For centuries, Maltese have been the cherished pets of royalty, socialites, divas and film stars. Actress Elizabeth Taylor has always been devoted to the breed, even keeping her dogs on a private yacht while she filmed in England. Hotelier and businesswoman Leona Helmsley left a fortune in her will to her pet Maltese, ensuring that the dog would want for nothing after her owner passed. Such is the loyalty that this refined, immaculate toy breed inspires.

The Maltese is single coated, with long, flat, silky white hair practically reaching the ground. The hair on the dog's head may be tied up in a topknot or left hanging. While a Maltese's full coat flowing around the show ring is a breathtaking sight, his owner must invest many hours each week in grooming to achieve that pristine result. Most owners keep them in a more manageable puppy cut, which gives their dogs the freedom to play on carpets and grass.

While the Maltese appears fearless, at 4 to 7 pounds this breed isn't appropriate for young children who could accidentally injure the dogs without meaning to. For older, gentle children, the Maltese can make a loving companion.

The breed's universal popularity is understandable. The Maltese is a charming and gentle creature, among the sweetest of all little dogs.

Allan Reznik
Editor-at-Large, DOG FANCY

SMALL BUT

MIGHTY

The Maltese's popularity is essentially a tried-and-true recipe. For centuries, these delightful little dogs have been cherished and refined, making them premier companions. The Maltese's best features aren't just his irresistibly adorable appearance. You may find yours to be a surprise package if you were expecting nothing more than a pretty bit of arm candy. Maltese may be one of the world's smallest breeds, but they are also undeniably athletic, bold and courageous. The Maltese's personality definitely does not take a backseat to looks.

MALTESE PERSONALITY

If you are lucky enough to spend any time with a Maltese, you will quickly discover that his presence is a perfect remedy for boredom or sadness. Maltese have no intentions of being ignored. They will employ some ingenious methods to prevent it, raising your spirits and entertaining

Did You Know? **The Maltese has a profuse coat.** It requires considerable grooming, and Maltese owners need to be willing to spend time brushing their dogs. If you're not planning on showing your Maltese, consider keeping her in a puppy cut. Five minutes with a brush and a quick wipe of the eyes each day can keep a pet Maltese looking spiffy.

you in the process. This might include anything from an impromptu play session to an affectionate cuddle that you didn't realize you needed.

This doesn't imply that Maltese crave nonstop attention and reassurance. The typical Maltese won't have any trouble keeping himself occupied, although he will likely ensure that you are never bored in the process. As long as he is with you, he can be equally happy hiking in the woods or acting as a bed warmer.

The Maltese is an excellent choice for urban dog lovers, but these versatile little dogs can adapt to a tremendous range of lifestyles — if you are prepared to provide daily care, attention and exercise. The Maltese is not a delicate little flower.

If given the opportunity, a Maltese will happily reveal the full extent of his athletic and intellectual prowess. They have demonstrated their talents at competitive dog sports ranging from agility to tracking. Even more surprising is the breed's talent as a watchdog. A Maltese will not hesitate to sound the alarm or defend his territory (or owner) against any threat. His repertoire of canine instincts also includes a strong predatory drive. Historical accounts of the breed include many descriptions of their skill as vermin hunters. However, this drive is usually expressed today through exuberant playfulness, such as hunting squeaky toys.

Maltese are very eager to please, but natural instincts can leave them easily distracted. Their prey drive and other canine instincts can complicate training. Maltese are keenly sensitive to social disapproval. Lessons must be kept frequent, short and upbeat. Consistency is the key to training, but you should avoid strict, repetitive training that will make your Maltese bored.

Don't assume that a small dog, like the Maltese, doesn't require training or can't benefit from it. A spoiled, ill-mannered pet is no fun to live with. More importantly, it is your responsibility to implement rules that are in your dog's best interest. Your Maltese will be far more secure and well adjusted if he understands your rules. The first step in training is to teach a puppy the meaning of the word "no." Teach him things like not to profusely bark, bite or fuss while being groomed. A stern verbal reprimand is sufficient to get your point across. Your dog will take his behavioral cues from you, who he'll consider his pack leader. If you are overly permissive or reluctant to set rules, he will quickly take advantage.

INTERACTING WITH OTHER FAMILY PETS

Maltese are naturally sociable and typically have no problems accepting other pets, but that doesn't imply that supervision is not required. Potential complications must be carefully considered before introducing a Maltese into your home menagerie. Some species are instinctively fearful or defensive toward dogs. Large reptiles and birds can do quite a bit of harm to a tiny dog if they feel threatened. If your Maltese has not been socialized as a puppy toward small-mammal species like hamsters and gerbils, he may perceive them as prey. In some instances, keeping such pets permanently separated is the safest course of action. Even if your pets do hit it off and get along with each other, your Maltese should be kept away from their food and sleeping areas to prevent territorial disagreements.

In most cases, introducing a Maltese to the family cat goes smoothly, but the

Meet other Maltese owners just like you. On our Maltese forums, you can chat about your toy dog and ask other owners for advice on training, health issues and anything else about your favorite dog breed. Log onto **DogChannel.com/Club-Maltese** for details!

outcome depends on a couple of factors. Dogs' personalities are typically more gregarious than cats, and some cats really have no interest in making friends with dogs. If your cat happens to have an independent nature, your efforts aren't likely to change that. Insisting on socializing the two pets will probably make matters worse. A defensive cat can seriously injure a small dog.

The outcome also depends on whether your Maltese has had any previous exposure to cats; this will make things easier but isn't essential. It isn't unusual for some dogs and cats to develop strong friendships, although it may not happen quickly. Don't become discouraged. You may need to host daily supervised visits for a week, a month or longer.

Either way, a carefully supervised gradual introduction process can prevent a lot of problems. Dogs and cats may easily misinterpret each other's signals, resulting in unintentional provocation. For instance, rolling over is a friendly playful gesture from a dog's point of view, but a cat might see this as an intention to fight. Even if they seem friendly toward each other, carefully observe their expressions and body language for indications of fear or aggression; always make sure the cat has a handy escape route if the introductions don't go as planned.

Forethought is also essential if you intend to bring a Maltese into your home as a companion for another dog. Maltese are a very friendly, nonaggressive breed, but even friendly play can lead to tragedy. A tiny dog can be seriously injured if a large dog pounces on or bites him during roughhousing. A Maltese isn't the best choice as a companion for a large or rambunctious dog.

If you do plan to introduce a Maltese into your pack, arrange to keep the animals separated when they are unsupervised until you are certain they will get along together. This may take weeks or months. No matter how friendly they seem when you're home, don't assume they will get along well when you aren't present. When first introducing dogs to each other, keep them on lead or separated by a barrier such as a baby gate. Gradually let them get close enough to sniff each other and physically interact. End the visit if either dog becomes aggressive, fearful or overly excited. You must pay attention to each dog's facial expressions and body gestures to understand what they are thinking and predict their behavior during initial encounters. They may be getting along fine one minute, but that can change instantly.

Most dogs enjoy having canine companions, and they probably will develop friendships with other dogs in the home. Don't meddle in the process. Your efforts to speed things up can undermine the socialization process's success. Forcing dogs to share beds, food or toys can instigate rivalries and dominance problems. Most importantly, give them time. It can take three or four weeks for a bond to develop between unfamiliar dogs.

INTERACTING WITH CHILDREN

For many reasons, Maltese usually aren't considered a good choice as companions for young children. Even an adult Maltese can be seriously hurt if accidentally dropped or stepped on by a child; a puppy weighing just a few ounces can be fatally injured. Aside from the possibility of accidental injury, children can't be expected to manage the routine care this breed requires.

Maltese are small enough to ride in a purse but too big to fit in your pocket!

Within the written breed standard, one finds a collection of words that describe the ideal Maltese temperament: fearless, playful, lively, vigorous, trusting and gentle. All bound up into one phrase, I would characterize the ideal Maltese temperament as "charming and endearing." Though they all have individual nuances that make them each distinctive and unique, they are all packaged into a little bundle of personality traits that indeed charm you to the point where you can't help but love them for just being themselves.

— breeder Angela Stanberry from New Orleans, La.

Toy dogs are not appropriate for little kids. The American Maltese Association advises parents that, although Maltese love children, they don't always make the best pets for children too young to understand that these dogs can be seriously hurt by rough handling. According to the AMA, if you have a very young child and plan to add a Maltese to your household, be careful to supervise their time together and teach the child that the fragile build of the Maltese calls for gentle care.

Parents often use pet care as a means of teaching responsible behavior to their children, but some breeds are more challenging than others. Properly caring for a Maltese requires fairly sophisticated judgment and skill. For instance, improper grooming can result in a coat-care disaster in a very short amount of time. Both underfeeding and overfeeding can very quickly take serious tolls on a little dog. When exercising a toy dog in public places, the owner needs the ability to perceive potential dangers posed by traffic or larger, aggressive dogs. Although Maltese are not naturally aggressive, they won't hesitate to defend themselves if teased or frightened by children. Typically, Maltese breeders prefer to avoid placing dogs in homes with children younger than 12 years old.

Of course, these are general recommendations, and many young children are thoughtful, gentle and careful. Even if you think your child is ready for such responsibility, be prepared with a game plan. Many parents prefer not to allow their children to carry the small dogs to prevent potential accidents. It's probably safest to have the dog and the child sit on the floor during their first introduction. Naturally, the child may want to hold or cuddle the dog, but that can immediately lead to problems if the dog is resistant or if the child is unable to securely hold the dog.

Whether they are puppies or adults, small dogs that haven't been raised with children need time to get accustomed to kids' behaviors and mannerisms. Children can seem intimidating to dogs — especially tiny ones — because their behaviors are so different from adults'. Loud, abrupt or unpredictable gestures can be mistakenly interpreted as threats, prompting anxiety and defensiveness.

Most importantly, ensure that you have sufficient time and patience to provide adequate supervision while your child and Maltese interact. If you already feel stressed and overworked with the demands of parenthood, adding a pet to the chaos is not a good idea. Even if your child is reliable, there will be occasions when other children come to visit and want to play with your Maltese, requiring even more vigilance on your part. Be prepared to spend time teaching your child and your Maltese proper rules for interacting with one another.

Don't expect a child to realize that some forms of play are too rough, frightening or potentially dangerous for a tiny dog. Kids can learn to behave calmly and gently when handling Maltese, but it takes time and practice. Regular play sessions are essential to this process, but they can also be a major source of trouble if you don't supervise them adequately. Your child must understand that it's never OK to grab, chase or corner a dog for any reason. If the dog needs to be disciplined, it should always be your responsibility; never leave it to a child. It's also important that a child be taught to respect the dog's need to retreat and understand that he is off-limits when resting or eating. A crate will definitely make things easier. Many parents prefer designs with complicated child-proof latches.

PHYSICAL CHARACTERISTICS

The Maltese is one of the dog world's most immediately recognizable breeds. Foremost among these trademark traits is his silky mantle of dazzling white hair. It is classified as a silky-textured coat, meaning straight, fine-textured hair without an undercoat. When properly textured and groomed, the Maltese's coat will grow to floor length. The ideal Maltese color is pure white with no traces of tan or lemon coloring. This dramatic feature is further enhanced by contrasting jet-black eyes and pigmentation. The Maltese's typical expression is irresistible because it's simultaneously sweet and mischievous. It perfectly reflects the breed's natural sensitivity,

A big bundle of attention in a little package, the Maltese loves to be close to her owner.

vitality and responsiveness. People fall in love with the breed's sparkling dark eyes, delicate tapered muzzle with black nose and lips, and softly framed and heavily feathered low-set ears.

Diminutive size and daintiness are other features that help accentuate peoples' ethereal perception of the Maltese. Ideally, a Maltese should weigh 4 to 6 pounds, never more than 7. While not the tiniest breed of dog, he's definitely among the smallest. Petite as he may be, he is noted for his sturdiness and verve.

It's possible to find Maltese weighing more or less than 4 pounds because size variation will occur in even the best breeding programs. Serious breeders normally exclude improperly sized dogs from their breeding programs. Although they do not fit the requirements of the breed standard, they still make excellent pets. However, it pays to be cautious when selecting a puppy that is well below the preferred size range. Some Maltese puppies are guaranteed to weigh less than 2 pounds when fully grown, and they are wrongly often referred to as "mini," "teacup" or "pocket" size. This is not an officially recognized classification, nor is it considered an especially prized trait. Serious breeders never intentionally breed to produce dogs outside of the preferred size limits. Although many undersized Maltese are healthy, they are known to be extremely fragile and may suffer from associated health problems.

EXTRACURRICULAR ACTIVITIES

It is tempting to treat your Maltese as a delicate work of art, but this isn't in his best interests. He is all dog, from the tip of his nose to the end of his tail. Don't just keep him cooped up at home all day or in a dog carrier or your purse when you take him out. His life will be much more enjoyable if you give him the chance to reach his full potential. This includes providing fun doggie activities including regular outings to the beach or the park. It might also mean introducing him to canine therapy work or competitive dog sports. You'll never know where his talents lie unless you give him a chance to try.

EXERCISE AND OUTDOOR ACTIVITIES

Although the Maltese has modest exercise requirements, daily outings are still essential to his well-being. It's possible to housetrain a Maltese to eliminate on newspaper or to use a litter box, but that doesn't offset the need for daily outdoor exercise. In some ways, a structured exercise routine is even more important for small dogs to maintain good muscle tone, build endurance, and prevent cardiovascular disease and weight gain. Tiny dogs are prime candidates for obesity.

Fortunately, you can easily ensure that your Maltese gets a daily workout; these dogs absolutely love toys and games. Daily play sessions aren't just fun for both of you;

> **it's a Fact**
>
> **The Maltese breed standard describes the Maltese temperament as fearless, trusting and affectionate.** "He is among the gentlest-mannered of all little dogs, yet he is lively and playful, as well as vigorous," according to the breed's standard. The Maltese is certainly all that and more.

Maltese are very affectionate and get their greatest enjoyment from being with you. They like to be really close, mostly in your lap if you let them. Because they are so small and sweet, many owners baby them, often taking them everywhere with them, carrying them in purses from place to place and fussing over them. I have often heard it said that: 'If you want a baby, get a Maltese, but if you're looking for a dog, look elsewhere.' — Paula Feig, owner of two Maltese in Sherman Oaks, Calif.

Maltese are typically gentle, placid dogs that have a great reputation for getting along with other pets in the household. However, this depends on the particular pet. Since Maltese don't have a strong hunting instinct like dogs that were bred to stalk or chase prey, they often can be safe friends with smaller animals like rodents, reptiles or birds. For the safety of the smaller animals, though, always supervise when your Maltese and other pets interact.

they also provide mental and physical benefits. It's the best way to teach a puppy the appropriate rules of human/canine interaction. It also fosters good communication and mutual trust, prevents boredom and gives your dog something to look forward to each day. Don't assume that a bored, frustrated Maltese can't conduct an effective reign of terror just because he happens to be small.

MALTESE MAYHEM

If your Maltese doesn't turn out to be a great fan of dog parks, play dates might be a better alternative. These can range from one-on-one visits with a friendly neighbor dog to large public gatherings of multiple Maltese owners. These get-togethers have become quite trendy for popular breeds in major cities. They give the dogs an opportunity to socialize with their peers. People also enjoy the chance to compare notes with other Maltese owners, take pictures and spend time with the breed they love. These events are usually publicized through online mailings or breed-related chat lists. Some have become truly gala affairs conducted as fundraisers for community groups or breed rescue organizations. Typical festivities might include dog and owner look-alike contests, costume shows or dog walks for charity.

THE FASHION-FORWARD MALTESE

A recent American Kennel Club survey revealed that 49 percent of dog owners enjoyed the idea of dressing up their pets. Don't be too quick to write this off as merely a silly pastime. Canine fashion shows and beauty pageants have become one of the most popular features of charity fundraisers. If you enjoy dressing up your Maltese and he enjoys showing off his wardrobe, why not put the hobby to good use? Try organizing a costume show or canine beauty pageant to raise donations for your local animal shelter or Maltese rescue group.

There is no question that Maltese are well suited to stylish couture. Quite a few doggie retailers cater to Maltese accessories, from gorgeous handmade topknot bows to dazzling tiaras and rhinestone collars. For other breeds, satin coats and deluxe pet carriers may seem frivolous, but they really are necessities for a well-appointed Maltese. Satin is the preferred fabric for canine coats and beds, not because the fabric looks so luxurious — which it does — but because it's the least likely to cause coat damage. When choosing accessories for your Maltese, safety and comfort should be as much a priority as style. Hair ornaments and collars should be free of sharp edges that could catch in the coat. Coats should be comfortable and well tailored to prevent chafing seams and to

allow for unrestricted movement. Pet strollers or dog
carriers should be sturdy
and secure to keep the
dog from falling or
jumping out.

However, never lose
sight of the fact that
your Maltese is a dog,
not a fashion accessory or
a status symbol. Showing
off your pet is one thing,
but treating him like an
inanimate object is quite
another. Dressing your
dog up or buying him
expensive accessories is
never a substitute for daily
care and training. Having an
adorable little dog may often
be the perfect icebreaker in
social situations, but check
whether dogs are welcome
before bringing your Maltese
along to shops, restaurants
or business meetings.

The Maltese's beauty,
cleanliness and
portability make
her a wonderful
companion.

Show your artistic side. Share photos, videos and artwork of
your favorite breed on Club Maltese. You can also submit
jokes, riddles and even poetry about Maltese. Browse through
our various galleries and see the talent of fellow Maltese owners. Go to **DogChannel.com/Club-Maltese** and click on
"Galleries" to get started.

Therapy Workers

The qualities that have made the Maltese a perpetual favorite in TV and films also shine on a more personal level. This is a wonderful breed for therapy work. Without formal training or credentials, Maltese have provided indispensable cheer and comfort to humans for centuries. In recent decades, the medical community has taken notice of the value of this service.

The therapeutic value of canine affection is scientifically documented. More than just entertainment or moral support, studies have shown that petting a dog triggers the release of the hormone oxytocin, which has a comforting effect on the dog as well as the person. It reduces stress and depression, lowers blood pressure and releases brain chemicals that foster a sense of well-being. Regular contact with a dog can speed recovery and enhance a person's motivation. Many nursing homes, hospitals and rehabilitation centers have implemented programs to provide patients with regular access to therapy dogs. These visits raise patients' morale and hasten their recovery. Patients pet, talk to, groom or walk the dogs, and many freely admit that they look forward to seeing the therapy dogs more than seeing human visitors.

Small, minimally shedding breeds with calm, tolerant temperaments are best suited for therapy work. For the Maltese, it can be an ideal career. Prerequisites for canine therapy work include basic obedience training and Canine Good Citizen certification. Additional training and certification is handled by local chapters of canine therapy groups. Contact these organizations for information regarding training and certification programs for therapy work. See Chapter 13 for more information.

At such a precious age, the Maltese pup is cute, yet she's also very delicate and fragile. Handle with care!

THE MALTESE MISSIVE

Small and sociable, the Maltese is the perfect go-anywhere breed.

COUNTRY OF ORIGIN: Malta

WHAT HIS FRIENDS CALL HIM: Malted, Prince, Snowball, Fluffy

SIZE: height — 5 to 8 inches; weight — under 7 pounds; 4 to 6 pounds is preferred

COAT & COLOR: Maltese are known for their long, pure white coats that part down the middle from their heads to their tails, with topknots on their heads. Owners can also keep them in a lower-maintenance puppy cut.

PERSONALITY TRAITS: Affectionate and playful, Maltese love spending time lounging around the house with their owners. They're social and self-confident but can be nippy with strangers or in situations that make them anxious.

WITH KIDS: Because of their tiny size and frail features, Maltese do best with older children. Breeders often prefer to place them in homes with kids at least 12 years or older.

WITH OTHER ANIMALS: Naturally sociable creatures, Maltese must be reminded of their small stature. If introduced properly, they get along well with other pets, but supervise their interactions with larger animals. Large reptiles and birds, in particular, can severely injure them.

EXERCISE NEEDS: moderate

GROOMING NEEDS: The breed's long, silky coat can become matted easily. Brush it thoroughly at least every other day to keep it nice and smooth. Clean around the eyes daily to avoid tear staining.

TRAINING ABILITY: Obedience train your Maltese puppy early in life, and you'll have a lifelong companion. Set household rules and follow a consistent daily routine to keep him happy. If you don't assert yourself as the pack leader in your home, your dog certainly will.

LIVING ENVIRONMENT: Although they're great for apartment–dwelling owners, Maltese also don't mind living in larger accommodations.

LIFESPAN: 12 to 14 years

CHAPTER 2

FROM MALTA,

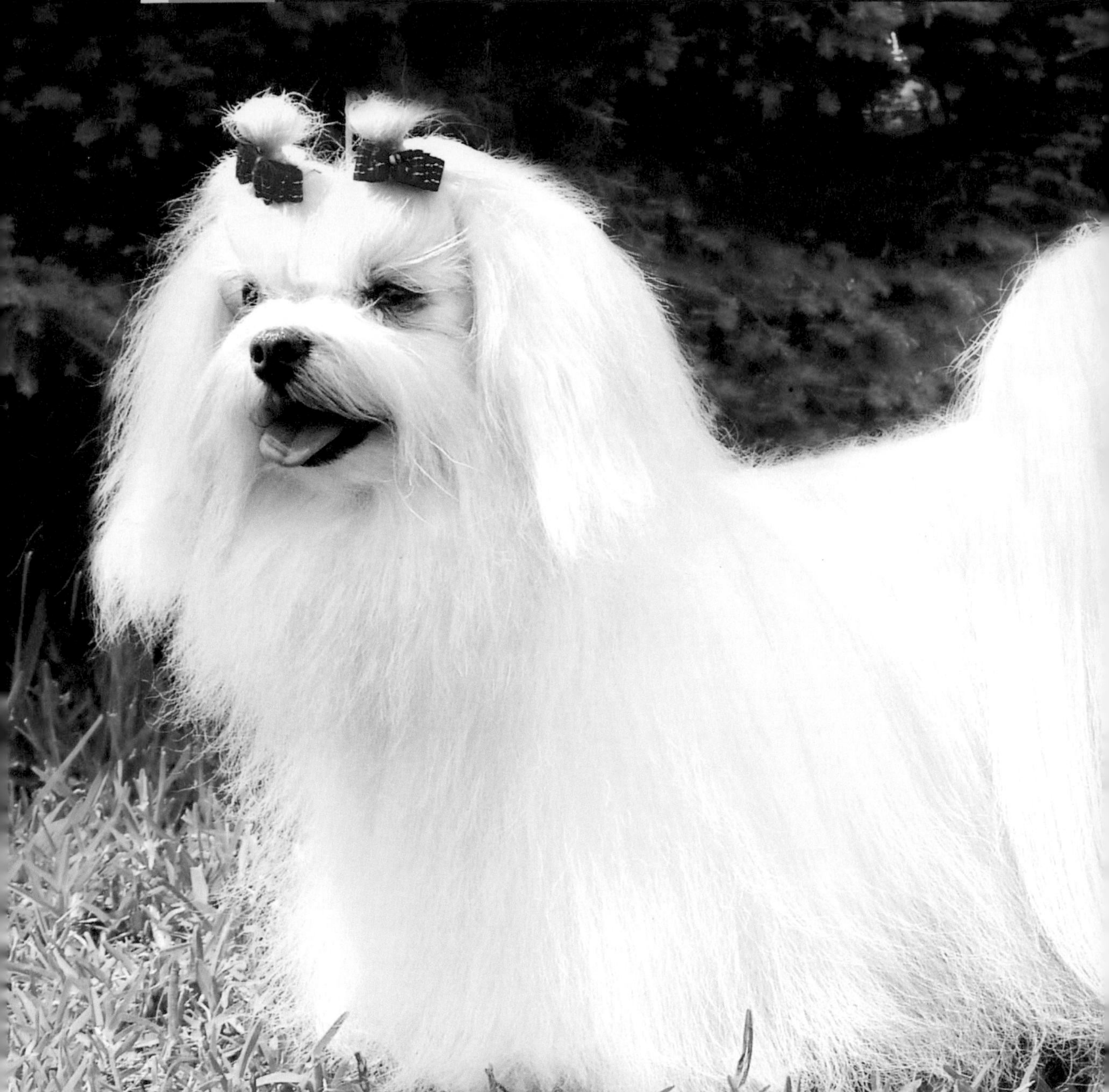

WITH LOVE

Little white lap dogs have been popular pets throughout recorded history. People in ancient times may have primarily considered dogs as utilitarian necessities, but archeological evidence shows that small pet dogs existed in old *and* new world cultures. Nowhere were they more celebrated than in ancient Rome. In addition to being noted dog lovers, the Romans were skilled animal breeders and meticulous recordkeepers.

Author Walter Hutchinson wrote in *The Dog Encyclopedia* (1935), "It was a favorite in the time of Phidias, and a pet of all the great ladies of Rome." However, there's no definitive proof that these little dogs were the actual ancestors of the modern Maltese. Small size and a profuse coat were two common features of a desirable lap dog, but they

Malta was the ideal starting place for the little Maltese to conquer the known world. Settled by the nomadic Phoenicians in approximately 1500 B.C., Malta was an important center of trade in ancient times, and dogs were an important item of barter. They were easily portable (especially if they were small, like the Maltese) and highly valued for various factors such as working ability, ferocity and novelty. It's no surprise the Maltese fell into the novelty category.

it's a
Fact

existed in a variety of types of dogs from divergent origins. As demand arose, a wide range of small, fluffy white dogs were likely bred in Malta and/or Melita and exported to all parts of Europe. The noted canine historian of the 19th century, James Watson, voiced his skepticism about a possible link between ancient and modern Maltese. In *The Dog Book* (1906), he noted, "Every writer goes back to Strabo and his remark about the dogs of Melita, Sicily, but merely saying that dogs came from Melita in his days and for us to call a dog 'Maltese' by no means carries any weight in supposing that our white toys were what Strabo referred to. They may be, but there is nothing to prove they are."

Historians believe that early Maltese ancestors probably arrived in England during the Roman conquest of the British Isles. By the Middle Ages, the Maltese became an established breed in England and Europe. Many accounts say that Queen Elizabeth I (1533-1603) and her arch nemesis Mary Queen of Scots (1542-1587) — one of history's great dog lovers — owned Maltese. The Maltese was one of many breeds that Queen Elizabeth helped to popularize.

Although ample evidence shows that European aristocracy adored Maltese as pets, the breed never became very widespread or popular during those centuries. One historian speculated this was due to the challenges of keeping them clean and well groomed. In *Histoire Naturelle*, (1767) Louis-Jean-Marie Daubenton speculated, "These dogs were very fashionable a few years ago, but at present are hardly seen. They were so small that ladies carried them in their sleeves. At last they gave them up, doubtless because of the dirtiness that is inseparable from long-haired dogs, for they could not clip them without taking away their principal attraction." More likely, the luxury of keeping lap dogs as pets was simply beyond most peoples' economic reach.

Most experts agreed that, by the 19th century, the Maltese was a rarity both in Europe and in its native land. Gordon Stables wrote in *Ladies' Dogs as Companions* (1879), "Although the best specimens have come to us in this country from Malta, you shall not find them growing on trees even in that sunny island. Indeed, they are quite as uncommon there as an honest gondolier."

EARLY ENGLISH IMPORTS

Several 19th-century canine authorities reported that two Maltese, Cupid and Psyche, were imported into England in 1841. The breed must have been quite rare by that time to excite such interest. Story has it that, while he was working for the East India Trading Company, a man named Captain Luckey purchased the pair in Manila. At the time, the trading companies commonly conducted a lucrative side business importing and exporting valuable dogs. English hunting and fighting dogs were in high demand worldwide. Likewise, European dog fanciers were fascinated by exotic canine rarities. Shippers were practically guaranteed substantial financial compensation if they were able to keep their canine charges alive and in good condition during their lengthy voyages. But that was easier said than done.

Although the Maltese has never won Best in Show at Westminster, she has several Best of Group wins amongst the Toys.

There is among us another kind of highbred dog ... which Callimachus called 'Melitei' from the Island of Melita ...

That kind is very small indeed and chiefly sought after for the pleasure and amusement of women. The smaller the kind, the more pleasing it is; so that they may carry them in their bosoms, in their beds and in their arms while in their carriages.

— Johannes Caius, English dog authority and physician to Queen Elizabeth, in his book De Canibus Britannicus, *published in 1570*

Cupid and Psyche were originally intended as gifts for the dog-loving Queen Victoria (1819–1901); however, their dirty, matted condition on arrival prompted a change of plans. Instead, Captain Luckey gave them to his brother, an experienced dog breeder, which proved fortuitous for the breed. He mated the pair, and their offspring served as foundation stock to establish some of the earliest Maltese bloodline in England. Of course, the fact that these dogs came from the Philippine Islands rather than from Malta caused some confusion for breed historians.

One of the pair's most famous puppies was also named Psyche. Her owner Miss Gibbs of Morden frequently showed her, and she became a main attraction at early Victorian dog shows. Psyche was described as weighing 3 1/4 pounds, with a 15-inch long coat. The breed was certainly viewed as an exotic rarity at the time. Psyche was immortalized in a portrait by Sir Edwin Landseer entitled "The Last of the Tribe." In *The Dog Encyclopedia*, Hutchinson wrote, "In the time of Sir E. Landseer, the breed was so scarce that he painted one as the last of the race. This was in the year 1840 or thereabouts."

CLASSIFICATIONS

Maltese were among the first breeds exhibited at early dog shows in the 1860s and 70s, which proved to be a vital step in rekindling interest in the breed and attracting new fanciers.

Naturalist and animal author Brian Vesey-Fitzgerald recounted the breed's growth in popularity in *The Book of the Dog* (1948), writing, "The Maltese is, by no means, a common breed, yet neither is it really scarce. It has been carefully and devotedly led along since its early days in Britain as a fancy through several difficult periods, and is today a naturalized Toy Dog of long standing. Its show career in Britain began almost as early as did genuinely open dog shows themselves, that is, a little after the middle of the last century, and it enjoyed a very respectable support by the turn of the century."

Uncertainty regarding the breed's actual origins, however, resulted in classification problems at early dog shows. For instance, 19th-century show records indicate William McDonald's Maltese named Prince was exhibited in the "Foreign dog class" at the 1863 show in Birmingham, England. Such discrepancies hindered the Maltese's popularity and created mass confusion about the breed's type.

Watson concluded that, "The name Maltese is of comparatively recent adoption, and a hundred years ago they were called 'shock dogs.' That is purely an English name, taken from the wealth of coat."

In 1873, The Kennel Club, England's premiere kennel club, officially designated the breed as the Maltese Terrier, and it was considered a terrier for many decades. This may have been partly due to the practice of crossing Maltese, Skye Terriers, Paisley Terriers, Clydesdale Terriers and Yorkshire Terriers. Several early British breeders bred and exhibited Maltese, Yorkshire Terriers and a number of other breeds considered related to one another, such as the Broken-Haired Scotch. Some of their pedigrees reflect common ancestors.

The Maltese is often sited as an ancestor of the Yorkshire Terrier, and there is no question that experimental breeding between Maltese and Yorkshire Terriers took place at some point in the 1890s. In addition to a long, straight silky coat, a Maltese cross would have contributed the smaller size and compact body proportions that early Yorkshire Terrier breeders sought to produce.

A few decades later, Watson noted that the experiments had a negative effect on the Maltese type. He concluded, "The mystery then, as now, was how Lady Giffard managed to grow such coats … her dogs had coats which swept the ground on each side, and pure white in color as the driven snow … An attempt has been made to introduce colored varieties. The Maltese dog was always one of the color breeds, a pure white dog. If that is correct, colored dogs can only be obtained by introducing foreign blood." Eventually, erroneous concepts of terrier ancestry were laid to rest, as was the idea of breeding multicolored Maltese.

In time, the theories of the Maltese's terrier origin were replaced by the belief that Maltese shared a common ancestry with spaniels. They were sometimes referred to as Maltese spaniels, and it's quite possible that early Maltese were sometimes crossed with small spaniels that were popular comfort dogs for many centuries. Watson and other canine authorities believed the Maltese was most closely related to the Bichon breeds, and some early dog authorities referred to the Maltese as a variety of Poodle or a member of the Bichon family.

Watson wrote, "As the toy dog to which has been given the name of Maltese has no

How was the Maltese developed? The breed probably traces its origin to a spaniel-type dog. Small dogs called Bichons were known in the Mediterranean basin for thousands of years. Essentially miniaturized water retrievers, they descended from the same type of dog that produced the Poodle and the Portuguese Water Dog, among others.

connection whatsoever with any branch of the terrier family, we drop the suffix which it is customary to add to the name. If a suffix was necessary, it should be poodle or to go still farther back it might be spaniel but never terrier."

Dog writer and judge Vero Shaw shared this sentiment in *The Illustrated Book of the Dog* (1881), writing, "According to the Naturalist's Library, the Maltese Dog (*Canis Melitaeus*), the Bichon or Chien Bouffe of Buffon, is the most ancient of the small Spaniel races, being figured on Roman monuments and mentioned by Strabo."

Since the sources of origin were impossible to verify, eventually both terrier and spaniel were dropped as suffixes, and the breed became known simply as Maltese. In *The Modern Dog Encyclopedia* (1949), Henry P. Davis concluded, "At various times, they have been called spaniels and terriers, with the latter name predominating in the U.S. and Canada. However, because it is obvious that a three-pound dog can hardly be used for sporting purposes, the majority of governing bodies now limit the name to Maltese Dog."

EARLY DOCUMENTED LINES

The modern Maltese may bear familial resemblance to the little white dogs of Malta, but theories about their origin remain just that. No documented breeding records exist to definitively trace the breed's lineage back to dogs imported from Malta, or anywhere else for that matter.

Robert Mandeville of Southwark is often cited as the founding breeder of the modern Maltese. He developed the most famous 19th-century strain of Maltese during the 1860s and made a heroic effort to promote the breed to the public.

According to *The Dog Book*, Watson wrote, "There is very little evidence to show that our dogs had any connection with those which originated on the island [of Malta], and it seems more likely that the English stock came from France. They have never been at all common, and if it had not been for Mr. R. Mandeville of London, it is probable that we would not have any Maltese dog. The starting point of the breed seems to have been a dog called Fido, owned by a man named Tupper. Mr. Mandeville bred his Lilly to Fido and got a Fido of his own. He also bred Fan to Tupper's dog and got another Fido, after which he bred from these Fidos and stuck to the name so that, in the first [English Kennel Club] stud book, we have five of the same name all owned by him and shown between 1864 and '72."

The first English studbook in 1873 listed 24 Maltese. Only the dogs descending from Mandeville's "Fido" strain were registered with pedigrees. Their carefully documented lineage was not their only advantage, as they were universally acknowledged as the finest specimens of the era.

"The first dog show class for the Maltese was given in London at the Agricultural Hall in 1862," according to *The Modern Dog*

Encyclopedia. Twenty Maltese were reportedly entered in the show. The origin of the 20 dogs is uncertain, but the breed must have earned a respectable following by that time to merit its own classes at such a large show. Mandeville exhibited his Maltese at all the major shows, winning top prizes and attracting new fanciers to the breed.

Shaw also noted Mandeville's contributions to the breed's popularity in *The Illustrated Book of the Dog*, writing, "From the years 1860 to 1870, [Mandeville] practically swept the board at the shows held in Birmingham, Islington, Crystal Palace and Cremorne Gardens. To this gentleman's Fido and Lilly we are indebted for many of the beautiful little dogs now in existence."

Two of the most influential early English breeders who acquired their Maltese stock from Mandeville were Bligh Monk of Coley Park, Reading, and Joshua Jacobs of Oxford. Jacobs bred the famous Ch. Pixie, a big winner at late 19th-century shows. Monk bred Ch. Mopsey, whelped in 1865 and later immortalized by the artist George Earl. Stables wrote, "Lovely as an Arab's dream was Mopsey, property of Mrs. Monk, Coley Park, Reading. This doggie had already made his mark at some of the great sows. Mrs. Monk, I ought to mention, is one of the principal breeders of Maltese. Lady Giffard too, possesses some rare specimens, and Mr. Jacobs, of Hedington, Oxford, likewise makes this breed a specialty."

Classifications and descriptions vary, but Maltese are documented in show materials dating since the late 1800s.

By far, the most famous 19th-century Maltese kennel was Red Hill, which was founded by Lady Giffard in 1874. Her Red Hill bloodline was based on dogs acquired from

Joshua Jacobs. She is often considered to be the founder of the modern breed, considering that Red Hill was the dominant Maltese bloodline from 1874 to 1898, and Lady Giffard was practically the only person consistently breeding and exhibiting them for two decades. Her most notable champion was Hugh, born in 1875. According to records, he weighed 4 pounds, 10 ounces, and his coat measured 11 inches in length.

"She continued for some years to buy the best [Jacobs] bred, until she had a wonderful collection," according to *The Dog Book*. "For many years, she was the only exhibitor of Maltese, and no one who ever saw the beautiful dogs shown in her name and the condition they were always shown in will ever forget them. When Lady Giffard retired, there seemed to be no one in the fancy, all having given up the impossible task of beating the Red Hill dogs."

Early breeders, including Mandeville and Lady Giffard, helped to establish a consistent, definitive type and elevated the Mal-

Did You Know?

The Maltese continued to be popular and highly valued, even after the fall of the Roman Empire. Two dogs, a male and a female, matching the description of "melitaei," were formally presented to the Chinese Emperor Kou Tzu around A.D. 620 as a gift from the Holy Roman Emperor in Byzantium. It's easy to see how Maltese made their way around the world and, no doubt, influenced the development of other toy breeds along the way.

tese' popularity. However, once they retired from breeding and exhibiting, the breed began to be altered in undesirable ways.

In 1905, Watson noted that the breed had changed drastically since the days when the Red Hill dogs dominated the show ring. "The new idea seems to be a Yorkshire Terrier sort of dog, but that was not the old sort at all," he wrote in *The Dog Book*. "They also seem to have got the dogs far too large. The present standard says not to exceed 12 pounds. Lady Giffard's Hugh weighed 4 pounds 10 ounces, was 7 1/2 inches at the shoulder and had an 11-inch coat."

Many authorities felt that the breed had seen its heyday in England. Fortunately, during those decades, many good dogs were exported to Canada and America, where they laid the foundation for the breed in North America. According to *The Modern Dog Encyclopedia*, "The breed increased in popularity until about 1880. It held its own until World War I and then began to die out in England."

The deprivations of WWI curtailed dog breeding and exhibiting to a great extent in Europe. Quite a few breeds came close to extinction during those years, including the Maltese. The Maltese Club of London disbanded, and most breeders were forced to give up. After the war, enthusiasts made efforts to reestablish the breed. Since Maltese had become so scarce, fanciers first sought to import dogs from Malta. Miss May Van Oppen (later known as Mrs. Roberts) of Harlingen Kennels in Barnet, England, personally traveled to Malta searching for new stock, but she was unsuccessful. Eventually, she was able to locate and import four females from Europe, which she used to revive the breed in Great Britain.

In his *Dog Encyclopedia*, Hutchinson wrote, "During the Great War, the breed

You have an unbreakable bond with your dog, but do you always understand her? Go online and download "Dog Speak," which outlines how dogs communicate. Find out what your Maltese is saying when she barks, howls or growls. Go to **DogChannel.com/ Club-Maltese** and click on "Downloads."

became practically extinct in [the United Kingdom], and the few that were available were so interbred that it was a danger to breed from them. This circumstance forced the writer to import new stock, and enquiries in Malta itself resulted in dogs nearly as big as sheepdogs being offered. Eventually some were secured from Holland and Germany — notably a very fine and small bitch, Harlingen Dolly, which, when mated to an English dog, did a great deal for the breed — and most of the dogs today can be traced in descent to the original Dutch or German stock."

A new Maltese Club was founded in Britain in 1934, and the breed's future finally seemed secure. Mrs. Roberts's breeding program produced several notable winners including Ch. Harlingen Emblem and Ch. Harlingen Snowman, winner of 50 first prizes and 14 challenge certificates.

EARLY AMERICAN DOGS

Despite the breed's popularity in Europe and England, Watson noted that the Maltese remained a relatively obscure breed in the late 19th-century American dog scene. The breed did, however, have a healthy following in Canada at the time.

"By 1913, there were fair classes of them at [Canadian] shows. The most powerful kennel of the period belonged to Mrs. H. E. Short of London, Ontario. The First Canadian champion was Highbury Snow Ball, born June 8, 1908 and imported to Canada from England by Raymond W. Gard of Toronto. Snow Ball won his championship in 1915." (*The Modern Dog Encyclopedia*, Henry Davis, 1949)

The catalog for the first Westminster dog show in New York City in 1877 contains the entry for a Maltese "Lion Dog." A Maltese Skye Terrier was exhibited at Westminster two years later. Then in 1888, the American Kennel Club studbook recorded its first

Maltese named Snips and Topsy, pedigrees unknown.

A few breeders imported Maltese and established breeding programs. The first American club formed in 1906, known as the Maltese Terrier Club of America. The first American Maltese specialty show took place in 1917. Despite these steps to encourage support for the breed, it remained a rarity in the American dog scene.

Early registration statistics clearly show how rare the breed was in America. Less than 1,500 Maltese were AKC-registered between 1888 and 1950. The first Maltese were registered with the AKC in 1888. After that, none were registered for another 13 years. Six were registered in 1902, all from the same breeder, and an additional 27 were added in 1912. Between 1914 and 1918, 200 Maltese were AKC-registered. By 1939, the Maltese had nearly become extinct in America. Only four were registered that year.

MALTESE IN THE 1950s

After World War II, the Maltese attracted more interest, due in part to various factors. The postwar economic boom had an energizing effect on every part of the U.S. dog scene. New people began entering the sport, with leisure time and money to pursue an interest in purebred dogs.

Two separate organizations formed to promote the Maltese in the 1950s: the National Maltese Club, which became the Maltese Club of America, and Maltese Dog Fanciers of America, which was headed by one of the era's most prominent breeders, Dr. Vincenzo Calvaresi. His beautiful dogs and dramatic style of presentation (handling and grooming) garnered a new level of interest on the breed. He campaigned for his Villa Malta dogs from coast to coast, creating legions of Maltese fans wherever he went.

These developments had a striking impact, and 1,240 Maltese were registered to the AKC in 1951.

AMERICAN MALTESE ASSOCIATION

On Dec. 3, 1961, the two breed clubs merged to become the American Maltese Association. Calvaresi was the club's first president. The AMA held its first meeting in New York City in 1963, in conjunction with the Westminster Kennel Club Dog Show. At the meeting, they addressed the critical task of revising the breed standard, which the AKC approved in 1964. The AMA held its first preliminary match in July 1963 in Pasadena, California, and its first formal match in Louisville, Ohio, in June 1964. By 1966, the AKC gave the club approval to hold its first national specialty. The show took place on June 11, 1966, at the Columbiana Kennel Club Show in Salem, Ohio, and it was judged by the famous breeder and judge William Kendrick.

By the 1970s, the breed achieved a level of popularity that it continues to enjoy today. By 1970, more than 4,000 Maltese were registered with the AKC. According to current AKC statistics, the Maltese was the 20th most popular breed in the United States in 2009.

The American Maltese Association also sponsors many programs including a national rescue program, an educational committee, a health committee, a breeder referral service and an awards program. Annual awards are given to: top producing sire and dam, top dam, top breeder, top obedience, and top junior showmanship winner.

The club also publishes a yearly official newsletter called *The Maltese Rx*.

PICK OF

Your first introduction to a Maltese may have come via a dog show, a chance encounter with a friend's pet or a picture in a dog magazine. However it happened, it sparked your desire to have one of your own. That's a perfectly natural reaction to this charming breed, but it isn't a guarantee that a Maltese is right for you. Hopefully, you followed up your initial interest with enough research to confirm this. In that case, you are aware of the responsibilities, as well as the pleasures, that come with raising a Maltese puppy.

Since you have had the forethought and willpower to make an informed decision about selecting this breed, it's only sensible to do the same when finding a puppy. Impulsive decision-making becomes an even greater danger at this stage of the process. Maltese aren't just cute and irresistible; they're also known for their longevity. It's one of the real advantages to making this breed your companion. Selecting a sound, healthy puppy will ensure that your Maltese is with you for as long as 14 years. And that fact, more than

Local dog shows are great opportunities to meet serious breed enthusiasts. Seek out Maltese exhibitors and introduce yourself. Don't expect to talk at length, though, because enthusiasts are usually busy grooming and showing their dogs in the ring.

it's a **Fact**

anything else, should make you realize how important it is to select the right one.

The Internet has become the foremost tool in the process. But there is no magic formula to help you find knowledgeable breeders and the perfect puppy. This is not a "one-stop shopping" process. Books, magazines and websites are all good starting points, but don't limit your research there.

False advertising is as old as history, so your research should include learning how to read between the lines of puppy ads. Commercially bred puppies are routinely sold through websites and classified ads, falsely touted as coming from legitimate breeders. These puppy sources are generally very accessible and often difficult to distinguish from genuine breeder ads. A major tip-off is if they streamline the buying process: You will not be faced with the prospect of waiting weeks or months for a puppy. They actively encourage impulse purchases such as buying puppies for Christmas or as surprise gifts. They accept credit card payments, guarantee immediate delivery and never ask questions about what sorts of homes the puppies can expect. They also don't provide any follow-up once a purchase is completed.

Of course, a lack of follow-up is a minor inconvenience associated with purchasing a commercially produced puppy. Far more worrisome is the fact that these puppies are bred strictly for profit. No effort is made to select quality bloodlines or screen breeding stock for health or temperament problems. Nor do these puppies receive adequate care, attention and socialization before being sold. Although most commercially bred Maltese puppies appear fine at the time of sale, those factors greatly increase the possibility that the puppies will develop behavioral or physical problems later on.

Finding good breeders can be challenging, but it isn't impossible. Veterinarians, trainers, groomers and local dog clubs may be able to help. Dog shows are an excellent place to meet such people. The American Kennel Club and the American Maltese Association also have referral pages to help you find breeders in your area (see Chapter 13 for contact information). Breeders endorsed by the AMA are generally well informed and have extensive experience evaluating and placing puppies. Because of the substantial investment they have made in their dogs, they are dedicated to finding the best homes for their puppies. They are also required to comply with the club's official member code of ethics. Take a few minutes to visit their website and view this document. Whether or not the breeder you choose is a member of the club, these guidelines emphasize what to expect from a legitimate Maltese breeder.

Once you have located Maltese breeders in your area, call and ask if you can visit. If they are considering placing one of their puppies with you, they will be equally interested in a personal meeting. Be suspicious of any breeders who are unwilling to meet you or let you see their dogs. Dog breeders are normally delighted to show off their life's work and talk about them endlessly.

Don't be surprised if a breeder checks your references and asks a lot of questions

it's a **Fact**

The typical Maltese litter size is only two or three pups. Buyers should beware that the breed standard does not include "teacup" or "pocket" sizes; standard weight is between 4 and 7 pounds.

As difficult as it is to not fall in love instantly, don't just get the first pup you see. Do your research first.

before inviting you over. Although it is often referred to as a kennel visit, in reality, you will likely visit someone's home. Treat the meeting with the courtesy you would give anyone when visiting their home, rather than treating it like a trip to the mall. Call if you are going to be late, and don't show up with a carload of unexpected friends and pets.

Don't visit more than one breeder per day, especially if any of the breeders have young puppies on the premises. You may inadvertently spread contagious diseases.

Champions or otherwise, don't expect the dogs to appear ready to step in the show ring when you visit. They'll most likely be lounging around the house, but they should at least appear happy, healthy and clean. Even if the breeder does not have puppies available now, ask to see the potential parents of an upcoming litter or to see dogs of related breeding. In many ways, this is even more helpful than viewing a litter of puppies. It will give you a much clearer idea of what to expect. Most importantly, try to see the mother. If she is pregnant or nursing a litter,

NOTABLE & QUOTABLE

Understand that these puppies need a lot of care, a lot of love and a lot of participation in their lives. They need to have people around that talk to them and teach them because they don't know anything. They have to grow up and learn what you want.

— breeder Ellie Merget of Norco, Calif.

she won't be looking her best. But you can still evaluate her size, facial features, structural soundness and basic temperament. If you don't care for the looks or temperament of the mother, it is unlikely that you will be satisfied with one of her puppies.

Be prepared to ask questions during the visit. The breeder has set aside time to answer them for you, and don't be surprised if you are expected to answer a few yourself. This sort of discussion is essential to ensuring a good match between puppy and owner. For one thing, the breeder will want to ascertain precisely what sort of puppy you are looking for. Given enough information, a breeder will make suggestions based on your lifestyle and plans for the puppy. Matching puppies and owners is an art. Experienced breeders have a definite advantage; they have watched and evaluated generations of their pups since birth. They can reliably predict how particular puppies' personalities will develop.

This selection process won't just be tailored to a buyer's lifestyle and expectations; it usually will also include different conditions depending on the type of sale. For instance, a pet puppy may be sold with limited (rather than full) registration and a contractual obligation to neuter him (or spay her) within a specified time. The associated guarantee will be limited to health. The sale of a puppy for show or breeding always includes much more detailed obligations and guarantees.

Pay attention to your breeder's suggestions; as the old saying goes, "Buyer beware." If you don't know what to look for, you could get into a lot of trouble.

SELECTING A MALTESE PUPPY

While popular assumption holds that 7 weeks is the ideal age to select a puppy, it's really not a good idea for several reasons. Seven weeks is an extremely vulnerable age for puppies, mentally and physically. Their maternal immunity has waned, and their immature immune systems are not fully functional. Even if they are vaccinated at this age, vaccine failure is not unusual. Although they may be weaned, they remain extremely dependent on their mothers emotionally. Interaction with the mother during this time represents an irreplaceable aspect of the puppy's socialization and education.

A reputable breeder usually won't send a Maltese puppy to his new home earlier than 12 weeks after birth, and some prefer to hold onto their puppies for even longer. This is done to ensure the puppy's health and welfare, despite increasing the breeder's time and work. Don't worry that older puppies will be deprived of training and socialization. Breeders routinely provide their puppies with socialization and introductory training during these weeks. By 12 weeks, puppies are weaned and protected by some vaccinations. They are also larger, sturdier and more emotionally mature — all of which gives them a definite

Ethical breeders encourage their buyers to meet the puppies' parents. If the parents are not available because they are busy showing or breeding, the breeder should be willing to show you pictures and answer questions regarding the sire's (father's) and dam's (mother's) temperament and health.

Did You Know?

Questions to Expect

Be prepared for the breeder to ask you some questions, too.

1. Have you previously owned a Maltese?

The breeder is trying to gauge how familiar you are with the Maltese. If you have never owned one, illustrate your knowledge of the breed by telling the breeder about your research.

2. Do you have children? What are their ages?

Some breeders are wary of selling a puppy to families with younger children.

This isn't a steadfast rule, and some breeders only insist on meeting the kids to see how they handle puppies. It all depends on the breeder.

3. How long have you wanted a Maltese?

This helps a breeder know if your purchase is an impulse buy or a carefully thought-out decision. Buying on impulse is one of the biggest mistakes owners can make. Be patient.

Join Club Maltese to get a complete list of questions a breeder should ask you. Click on "Downloads" at **DogChannel. com/Club-Maltese**

When selecting a puppy, be sure to pick up each one and get a good feel.

indication of a spindly, narrow body. The ribcage should be at least half the puppy's total body length, preferably more.

Observe the puppies running around on the floor. Don't be overly concerned about whether they respond to you or how they interact with each other. Just focus on observing the puppies' bodily movements. Puppies are normally uncoordinated. They will run, jump and pounce on each other, falling and rolling all over in the process. This should never include any signs of stiffness, pain, hopping, limping or disorientation while walking or running. A puppy should be able to bear weight evenly and comfortably on all four legs. His back should be straight with no rises or dips, and his tail should be held high.

Take a close look at the puppy's head and expression. His facial features should be perfectly symmetrical. Check the top of his skull for an opening or soft spot, especially if the puppy is small. A tiny soft spot is not that uncommon in small toy-breed puppies. It's generally found in the center of the forehead and is comparable to a human baby's open fontanel. A soft spot is not an indication of a neurological disorder; it usually closes by adulthood. However, a very large soft spot, bigger than the diameter of your fingertip, may be cause for concern.

Make sure the pup's nose and eye rims are completely black. His eyes should be evenly sized, uniformly dark, clear and bright. Reddish-brown hair discoloration beneath the eyes isn't uncommon in Maltese. It's not an indication of an eye problem.

Make sure his expression is curious and alert. His breathing should be quiet, relaxed and even, and his breath should be odorless. You should not notice any discharge from his nose or eyes. His ears should be pink on the insides, with no signs of irritation or odor.

advantage when coping with the stress of going to a new home.

Another advantage to waiting until a puppy is slightly older is that you'll be more able to predict adult traits such as size, facial features and coat quality. Unless you have a very experienced eye, viewing a litter of young puppies is a guessing game. Here are a few tips on what to look for:

Don't hesitate about picking up the puppies. You can't evaluate them otherwise. Pick one up and feel his structure beneath the coat. Puppies should have a rounded shape, not excessively fat and potbellied or thin and bony. You should be able to feel a sturdy little body beneath the coat. The puppy's ribcage should be nicely rounded, with no

Another way to acquire a Maltese is to adopt one from a shelter or rescue group.

Keep in mind that rescued dogs are likely to need a great deal of time and effort. Health or temperament issues may be the reasons they were consigned to a shelter in the first place, or problems may arise as a result of shelter life.

Shelter adoption fees usually include a health check, deworming, microchipping and vaccinations. You may be required to pay a license fee, but everything else should be covered by the adoption fee. Most, but not all, shelter dogs are neutered or spayed before being placed for adoption. For budgetary reasons, shelters usually aren't equipped to provide follow-up or support for new owners.

In contrast, rescue groups customarily provide excellent support networks for new owners. Those run by national breed clubs are known to have extensive support resources. They usually take dogs back if it is necessary at any time during the animal's life; however, they usually don't refund adoption fees. Rescues typically require thorough preadoption background checks before adding adoptees' names to their waiting lists. Foster caregivers get an opportunity to closely observe the dogs and address health or behavior issues that may not be immediately apparent.

In addition to getting the dogs vaccinated, dewormed and spayed/neutered, rescue groups also usually provide more extensive healthcare ranging from dental cleanings to heartworm treatments or major surgeries. By the time a dog is offered for adoption, the members of these groups have a major financial and emotional investment in the pet's welfare. Therefore, they often go to great lengths to avoid placing any dogs in the wrong homes where they may be mistreated, misunderstood or relinquished back to the rescue.

The American Maltese Association sponsors a national rescue network, as does the American Kennel Club. See Chapter 13 for contact information and other resources.

ADOPTING A RESCUE PUP

Head shaking or scratching can indicate an ear infection. His face should be evenly covered in a fur coat; thin, bare or scaly patches could indicate mange.

Check his teeth. Puppies begin shedding their puppy teeth at 4 months of age. Unless he is teething, he should have a complete set of puppy teeth, with six incisors on the top and bottom. His gums should be a healthy pink color.

The puppy's coat should be shiny and not too thick or fluffy, especially on the legs. A heavy coat may look adorable, but it is not any guarantee of good health and might not grow into a correct silky adult coat. An abundant coat is due to a heavy undercoat, which a well-bred Maltese should not have. The color should be white, with no obvious patches of color.

TEMPERAMENT EVALUATION

Temperament is a complicated blend of genetics and environment. Maltese temperaments can include a complete range of personality types from feisty to laidback. Some breeders utilize temperament tests, but they're not infallible, especially for young puppies. During the socialization period, puppies experiment with taking on many roles within their litter, acting dominant one day and submissive the next. Time of day, appetite and stage of life can all temporarily affect a puppy's personality. Temperament traits don't begin to stabilize until 3 or 4 months of age, and the puppies remain susceptible to many influences until adulthood. For instance, one sufficiently traumatizing experience can permanently alter a puppy's temperament, or a submissive puppy can start experimenting with opportunistic dominance if adopted by a passive, soft-hearted owner.

You can conduct informal testing simply by observing the puppies at play. Look for a calm, outgoing puppy that doesn't shy away. The liveliest puppy in the litter is usually the most eye-catching, but he can become a handful later on if he is too outgoing or aggressive. Likewise, the quiet and reserved puppy may need an owner who can dedicate extra time to socialization. Give careful thought to how each type of temperament might fit into your lifestyle.

■ How do the puppies interact with their mother and littermates?

■ Which ones are more dominant and fearless, and which are laidback or shy?

■ Place an unfamiliar object, such as a novel type of toy, in their midst. Which puppies boldly approach it to investigate? Which ones are more inclined to be suspicious or cautious?

■ How do the pups react to you?

It is not unusual for puppies to be somewhat reserved when first meeting a stranger. But they should overcome any initial shyness quickly with a bit of petting and encouragement.

SHOW SELECTION

If you have hopes of showing or breeding your Maltese, discuss this with the breeder

Ask the breeder which puppy he or she thinks will best suit you and your lifestyle.

Breeder Q&A

Here are some questions you should ask a breeder and the answers you want.

JOIN OUR ONLINE **Club Maltese™**

Q. How often do you have litters available?

A. You want to hear "once or twice a year" or "occasionally" because a breeder who doesn't have litters that often is probably more concerned with the quality of his or her puppies, rather than with making money.

Q. What kinds of health problems do Maltese have?

A. Beware of a breeder who says "none." Every breed has health issues. For Maltese, some genetic health problems include hypothyroidism, tracheal collapse and slipped kneecap (patellar luxation).

Get a complete list of questions to ask a Maltese breeder — and the ideal answers — at Club Maltese. Log onto **DogChannel.com/Club-Maltese** and click on "Downloads."

in advance. It will play a critical role in the selection process. Serious breeding programs are aimed at consistently reproducing the mental and physical traits necessary for these endeavors. It's a carefully achieved process, not done by happenstance.

Deciding you might want to show your puppy after you've picked a pet can lead to a big disappointment. Your puppy may look wonderful to you, but many breed imperfections are imperceptible to the untrained eye. There will be no guarantee that the puppy is up to the challenge. The breeder probably won't agree to a refund or replacement if you haven't agreed on these considerations in advance and covered

them in the sales contract. Purchasing a show puppy is just the beginning of a huge commitment of time and money. Months of training and conditioning take place before a show dog sets foot in the ring.

State upfront that you are looking for a prospective show or obedience dog, and the breeder will advise you on what traits to look for and at what age to evaluate them. In some cases, the breeder will not agree to guarantee a particular trait until a puppy reaches a certain age. The sales contract will include far more detailed quality guarantees than would be discussed in a pet sale. In addition to good health, the breeder will guarantee traits

Don't just choose a puppy based on her looks. She may be adorable, but pay attention to her personality, too.

like size, coat, dental alignment and ear carriage. Sound structure is equally critical for a show or obedience prospect. No matter how trainable or intelligent a puppy may be, he will not be able to face the challenges of competition if his shoulders or knees are badly constructed.

PEDIGREES, REGISTRATION CERTIFICATES AND OTHER IMPORTANT DOCUMENTS

Regardless of whether you are purchasing a show dog or a pet, at the time of the sale, you should expect to receive documentation regarding your puppy's health, care and lineage, as well as a contract describing the conditions of the sale, guarantees and return policies. Health records should cover vet exams, deworming and vaccinations that the puppy has received, in addition to a schedule for any other vaccinations, tests and treatments he needs. Common instructions should include feeding, grooming and general care. The puppy's transition to a new home will be far smoother if you adhere to the schedule he is accustomed to.

The breeder may provide a health certificate from a veterinarian or request that a vet examine the puppy within a stated amount of time after the sale. Most breeders permit puppies to be returned for full refunds for any reason within 48 hours of sale. If the puppy is found to be suffering from a health problem after that time, you may or may not be entitled to a refund or replacement depending on the terms stated in the contract.

If the registration papers are to be withheld or issued at a later time, this fact should be stated in advance of the sale. Otherwise, you should expect to receive either a registration certificate or application. Registration applications have one-year time limits, so don't stick yours in a drawer and forget about it. You will need to complete the form by filling in your information and the puppy's name (limited to 25 letters and spaces). The regular fee is $25. If it is submitted late, penalty fees may raise the cost to $50 or more. You will receive a registration certificate bearing your dog's unique registration number, his breed, sire (father) and dam (mother) information, birth date, sex, color, breeder and owner. The certificate does not include any endorsements of health or quality.

Purebred registries like the AKC limit their registrations to purebred puppies from purebred parents, but they do not regulate the quality of the dogs that are bred and registered. This is entirely the breeders' responsibility, and registration provides no assurance of breeders' business practices or the quality of dogs they produce. In reality, an unregistered puppy from a reputable breeder is likely to be far better quality than a fully registered puppy from a backyard or commercial breeder.

Don't confuse your dog's pedigree with his registration certificate; it is a separate document showing the puppy's family tree. The breeder may provide you with a copy of your puppy's pedigree from his or her own records, or you can order an official copy. Pedigree documentation is nice to have, but you really don't need to research it unless you plan to breed or show him.

PET INSURANCE

In the past decade, pet insurance has become a popular way to offset the expenses associated with owning a new puppy. It basically works like health insurance and similarly requires careful selection. Research the company and read the fine print on the policy before choosing a plan. Prices vary drastically. Plans that cover most basic routine services, like shots and checkups, usually have higher premiums; others only cover serious illness and injury. Most will not cover elective procedures or late-onset conditions due to hereditary defects. If you decide to get pet insurance for your Maltese, it is far more economical to buy it while he is a puppy.

WORTH THE WAIT

Maltese breeders who are members of the American Maltese Association agree to abide by a code of ethics, which includes a promise to keep puppies in their possession until 12 weeks of age. For breeders dedicated to the well-being of the Maltese, this is an easy promise to keep. To potential buyers, the idea of waiting until a puppy is 12 weeks can seem unnecessary. But truth be told, the recommendation is really in the Maltese puppy's best interest. Here's why:

The Maltese is a very small breed. When full-grown, adults only weigh about 4 to 7 pounds, meaning the toy breed's puppies are even smaller. Experienced Maltese breeders say the diminutive Maltese takes time to "come along" or mature. Weaning isn't hurried, and it takes time for these tiny pups with tiny mouths to manage eating solid food. It takes 12 weeks of age for the Maltese pups to thrive, both eating well and becoming somewhat independent.

Because of their small stature, it's extra important that Maltese puppies eat frequently during their first 12 weeks of life. Puppies that do not eat properly are prone to hypoglycemia, a condition in which the blood-sugar level drops too low. Hypoglycemia can cause seizures or a coma, which mean serious and expensive emergency veterinary visits.

Big changes in the home environment can also overly stress very young pups. So, if you contact a breeder who says he or she has puppies that aren't quite ready for adoption yet, be patient and be sure to thank the person for caring!

Healthy Puppy Signs

Here are a few things you should look for when selecting a puppy from a litter.

1. **NOSE:** It should be slightly moist to the touch, but there shouldn't be excessive discharge. The puppy should not be sneezing or sniffling persistently.

2. **SKIN AND COAT:** Your Maltese puppy's coat should be soft and shiny, without flakes or excessive shedding. Watch out for patches of missing hair, redness, bumps or sores. The pup should have a pleasant smell. Check for parasites, such as fleas or ticks.

3. **BEHAVIOR:** A healthy Maltese puppy may be sleepy, but she should not be lethargic. A healthy puppy will be playful at times, not isolated in a corner. You should see occasional bursts of energy and interaction with her littermates. When it's mealtime, a healthy puppy will take an interest in her food.

There are more signs to look for when picking out the perfect Maltese puppy for your lifestyle. Download the list at **DogChannel.com/Club-Maltese**

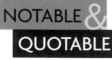

Buy from an established breeder, preferably a breeder who also exhibits. Exhibitors have reputations they must live up to. It isn't worth risking a well-built breeding and showing reputation just to turn a profit from the sale of an unhealthy or inferior pet. — breeder Barbara Bergquist of New Boston, Mich.

GOODS

Maltese don't travel light. Before bringing home a new puppy or adult dog, make sure you know exactly what supplies you will need. This is not simply a matter of running to the nearest convenience store for a squeaky toy and a bag of dog food. Nor should it be viewed as an opportunity to do a lot of poorly planned impulse shopping. If possible, get breeders' recommendations rather than resorting to trial-and-error experimentation. It will save you an enormous amount of time, money and confusion.

CRATE

One of the first things you'll need is a crate. For safety, you should always transport your Maltese in a crate. Be prepared to bring one with you when you pick him up from the breeder or rescue to take him home. Don't assume it is something you will only use once or twice and then stick in the closet. You will need a crate whenever your Maltese travels by car, such as to the veterinarian and to grooming appointments. A sturdy crate is indispensable for housetraining, too, and it is the best way to ensure your puppy is safe when you must leave him unsupervised.

Maltese and Brits go way back. The breed first appeared at dog shows in England in 1862, when 20 dogs were entered in the Holborn show in London.

it's a
Fact

A puppy should have her own space to relax, preferably a crate.

The most popular style is a small-sized plastic crate. These carriers are inexpensive, lightweight and easy to clean. They cost approximately $30 to $40 dollars and can be dismantled for storage if needed. Open-sided wire crates, which can be folded, are also handy. Some dogs prefer them, but many find them to be less cozy and secure. Collapsible plastic or soft-sided mesh crates are not recommended for puppies.

When selecting a crate, your primary considerations should be sturdiness, portability and ease of cleaning. The crate absolutely must be sturdy and secure, but it should also be light enough that you can conveniently carry it. Crates made of porous materials, such as wood, look attractive, but they cannot be disinfected. Once inside, the dog should be able to comfortably stand and turn around, with approximately 4 inches of headroom. If you are buying a crate to aid in your puppy's housetraining, don't choose a large one that he can "grow into." An overly large crate will totally defeat its purpose in housetraining. The point is to provide your puppy with a small enough space that he won't want to soil his current dwelling place. If the crate is too

Did You Know?

Throughout their history, in every land, Maltese have gone by many names: Melitaei, Ye Ancient Dogge of Malta, Roman ladies' dog, comforter, spaniel gentle, bichon, Maltese Lion Dog and Maltese terrier. Some of those names refer to personal characteristics — such as comforter and gentle — others refer to the breed's presumed place of origin. Still others try to place them in a breed category.

Maltese love to be where the action is. They're happiest spending time alongside whatever you are doing around the house.

large, the puppy may lose his inhibition and go in the crate. A large crate is also dangerous for travel because a small dog will be more easily knocked around if the crate is jostled or dropped.

BARRIERS

You will also need some kind of barrier to restrict your dog's access to certain parts of your home. Barriers are not only important for safety; they're also a critical aspect of the housetraining routine. Before you bring your puppy home, devise a plan for his daily routine, including where he will be expected to eat, sleep and eliminate. If he has free run of the house, he will likely choose his own spots for these activities — and probably in places you don't want him to go.

A puppy, or adult dog for that matter, will learn unwanted elimination habits within a day or two of his arrival, unless you take steps to prevent them. Limit your dog to a manageable amount of space so you can

Dog beds and crates should be placed in areas where people are. Maltese want to be near their owners, even when resting.

supervise him and he can find his way to his potty papers or the doggie door without complication. Barriers are also important for preventing your Maltese pup from wandering out of your house. Make sure the access points in and out of your house are always secure, regardless of your dog's age.

Keeping your puppy in a fenced yard is not a guarantee that the small dog won't be harmed or attempt to escape. Leaving a Maltese alone outdoors exposes him to the dangers of wild animals, large dogs, aggressive neighborhood cats or various other outside threats.

Maltese can't tolerate weather extremes for extended periods of time, either. Unlike many other breeds, Maltese do not grow a heavy winter coat in response to cold weather. This is not an outdoor breed. Relegating a Maltese to the backyard is not an acceptable means of restricting his access to your home.

Pressure-mounted doorway gates are handy for temporary restriction. Lightweight, plastic-coated, fold-up exercise pens (X-pens) are also handy. Make sure the bars are spaced together closely enough to prevent a Maltese from squeezing through or getting a foot or jaw stuck between them. You can also assemble a safe puppy pen using "baby

JOIN OUR ONLINE **Club Maltese™**

Before you bring your Maltese home, make sure you don't have anything that can put her in harm's way. Go to Club Maltese and download a list of poisonous plants and foods to avoid. Log on to **DogChannel.com/Club-Maltese** and click on "Downloads."

units," which are interlocking panels available at baby-supply stores.

BEDDING

Once you decide where your little Maltese is going to sleep, you'll need to provide him with a bed. You can find pet beds in styles ranging from utilitarian to opulent. Fancy beds are fine for trained adults but are not advisable for puppies. Look for sturdy fabrics with tight stitching that isn't prone to unraveling.

Puppies may be tempted to chew pillows and can ingest loose stuffing that is poking through frayed seams or small tears. Wood and wicker pet beds are also dangerous for these same reasons. Instead, consider purchasing a molded plastic pet bed, designed so that you can easily wipe it down with a disinfectant.

Be careful if you let your Maltese sleep in your bed. This is a common arrangement, but it can lead to problems. If you are a heavy sleeper, you may accidentally roll over on your Maltese or knock him out of bed. Keep in mind that young puppies can't

be expected to sleep through the night without needing a potty break. So be prepared to wake up and deal with this at least once during the night.

DISHES

You will also need a couple of small shallow, no-tip metal or ceramic dishes for your dog's food and water. Plastic dishes are not recommended for Maltese because they can trigger contact allergies or cause nose pigment discoloration.

CLEANING AND HOUSETRAINING SUPPLIES

Housebreaking pads, disinfectants and enzyme odor neutralizers are all housetraining essentials. Scrupulous cleanup isn't just important for obvious reasons. If you don't disinfect thoroughly after an accident, lingering traces of odor will constantly lure the dog back to that spot, making training more complicated.

Cleanliness is important, but try to use cleaners with natural ingredients instead of potentially toxic chemicals when possible. Trace amounts of chemicals on bedding or floors such as bleach, pine or oil-based products can trigger allergies or toxic reactions.

Newspaper is the traditional choice for indoor housetraining. It's highly absorbent and easy to find. But it is also perfect for turning a white coat a lovely shade of gray. Maltese breeders usually use rolls of unprinted newspaper because newspaper ink is surprisingly difficult to remove from white coats.

Absorbent housetraining pads are also popular for small breeds, but keep an eye on your Maltese when you first start using them. Some dogs love to tear the pads to shreds and can easily ingest pieces, causing

Having your Maltese sleep in your bed with you is an accident waiting to happen. She'll be better off in her own crate at night.

choking or intestinal obstruction. If you want to train your Maltese to always eliminate indoors, you can also try training with a litter box. Canine litter boxes are basically the same as feline ones, except they're filled with absorbent pellets. The same training and cleanup tactics apply for dogs as for cats, and you can dispose of waste at your convenience when you are home.

If you plan to train your Maltese to eliminate outdoors, you will need a collar or harness, a lead, and a pooper scooper or cleanup bags.

COLLARS AND LEADS

Small, lightweight collars and leads can be difficult to find, but they are essential to your Maltese's training and lifelong safety. Some breeders recommend using a cat collar if you can't find an appropriately sized dog collar. The collar should be flat, lightweight, made of nylon or leather, and wide enough to protect the puppy's throat. Fabric collars aren't as sturdy, and chain collars can pull the dog's hair or damage his coat. Very narrow collars can be sharp, which can potentially damage a puppy's neck.

Buckle collars are preferable to choke collars for the same reason.

When buckled, the collar should be snug enough to ensure that the dog can't slip his head out or get a leg or jaw caught inside it if he tries to get the collar off. A tiny, fine-boned dog like a Maltese can easily break a leg or jaw trying to free himself. Always remove the collar when your puppy is unsupervised or in his crate to avoid him getting caught and choking. As a rule of thumb, you should be able to slip two fingers between the collar and your Maltese's neck, but every dog has his own comfort zone. Your puppy will grow quickly, so you'll need to regularly adjust and replace his collars accordingly.

Many owners of small dogs, like the Maltese, choose to use harnesses instead of collars on their miniature pups. Puppies often accept them more readily, as a harness is less likely to irritate the dog's throat. When selecting a harness for you Maltese, look for a step-in design that doesn't encircle his throat. Proper fit is essential. Harness size is generally calibrated by measuring around the widest point of the chest (behind the dog's elbows) and adding two inches. However, this measurement is not fool-proof. Try the harness on your dog to ensure proper fit and freedom of movement without chafing.

Training a puppy to walk on a lead and harness is often easier than getting him to accept the feel of a collar, but a harness doesn't provide the same degree of control because it doesn't give control over the dog's head that way a collar does. Many dogs also exhibit a natural reflex to opposition, and they'll instinctively pull in the opposite direction that you try to take them. This is true of sled dogs and unruly pets alike. Whether you use a collar or harness, always

remove the device after you take your dog for a walk. Leaving it on may cause a skin irritation, mat the pup's coat or permanently affect a growing puppy's normal gait by stretching his shoulder tendons.

When you buy a lead, choose a lightweight nylon or durable leather one that is about 5/8-inches wide and no more than 6 feet long. Look for one with a small swivel snap, which will keep the leash from wrapping like a corkscrew during long, lively walks. Retractable leads are often too heavy for very small dogs, but that isn't the only drawback: A tiny dog can be seriously injured by an oncoming car or unwary pedestrian before you have time to retract the lead or even notice the approaching danger.

Pet carriers and strollers have become popular alternatives for toting small dogs

You must provide your Maltese puppy with a safe area where she can be left unsupervised. This might be an exercise pen or a partitioned area of a kitchen or laundry room. You can even use a crate, if you only use it for short periods of time. This won't work, however, if you plan to be gone for several hours. Nor can you expect your puppy to remain in a crate for eight hours at night. Figure out your new puppy's containment arrangements before bringing her home, especially if you expect her to sleep in this area. A puppy can get into a lot of trouble when left to wander through the house alone at night. Wherever you choose to contain your Maltese, be sure to stock the area with water, bedding, paper or a litter box for the pup to relieve herself, and a few toys to keep her occupied in your absence.

safely in congested pedestrian traffic. They are also perfect for taking your Maltese on public transportation. Even though carriers and stroller offer a greater measure of safety, you'll still need to exercise some common sense and pay close attention to your dog while using one. And make sure the product is safely and securely designed to prevent accidental escape or injury.

CLOTHING

As a Maltese owner, you might not need any prompting to invest in a sumptuous wardrobe for you pet. *Haute couture* is irresistible, but don't forget to choose a few practical cold-weather garments. For a coated breed like the Maltese, the choice of fabric is an important consideration. Heavy knit sweaters are popular, but they're not recommended for Maltese. Try one on for size, and you may discover that your dog has turned into a giant mat ball after a few hours of wear. Instead, look for blanket-type coats lined with smooth, satiny fabric. This will keep your dog warm, while protecting his coat at the same time.

TOYS

Maltese are notorious toy lovers. Even senior dogs often remain devoted to their favorite toys. Luckily, this breed isn't known for its destructive abilities. Most types of toys are safe for Maltese. Very often, household items like a knotted pair of old socks become lifelong favorites, as well as durable plastic squeaky toys and plush toys. Baby toys can also make great toys for Maltese. Unlike dog toys, ones designed for babies are safety tested. Dental chews and rawhides are fine for supervised play; they have the added benefit of helping to keep your dog's teeth clean. Regularly check all of your dog's toys for signs of damage and wear, then discard anything dangerous before he manages to remove any loose parts that he could accidentally ingest. Of course, there is no substitute for good supervision regardless of how safe any particular toy may be.

DOG-PROOFING

Obviously, it is impossible to vigilantly supervise a Maltese puppy at all times. You should plan to puppy-proof parts of your home and restrict your dog's access to others. Puppies certainly have no business wandering through garden sheds, storerooms or garages that often contain potentially dangerous items; so keep those areas off limits. A curious or bored puppy can get

There are so many fashionable products available for small dogs, but don't go overboard with the carrier purses and clothing. Remember to let your Maltese be a dog and walk and play on her own sometimes.

Maltese are easy to train if they understand what you want them to do because they love making their people happy. — breeder Linda Lamoureux of Anchorage, Alaska

into things that you can't imagine anywhere in the house. He might even ingest poisonous substances without you noticing. That is, until he falls ill suddenly for reasons you don't understand.

The easiest way to dog-proof your home is to confine your puppy to a pen or kennel when you can't supervise him. Doing so can keep him out of harm's way and keep you from having to constantly watch him while trying to do other things around the house. If left alone for long periods of time, though, this will also seriously undermine his training and socialization, making it impossible for him to fully integrate into your family pack.

As part of your puppy's ongoing socialization, it is vitally important to include him in your daily routine and to expose him to new experiences. It is also your responsibility to nurture his playfulness and natural curiosity within

safe bounds. A Maltese puppy cannot be expected to understand that something is forbidden or dangerous unless he is given opportunities to explore and learn about the world around him.

When you're puppy-proofing your house, keep an eye out for typical household dangers; cover electrical outlets, stow electric cords and place houseplants, medications and cleaning supplies out of reach. Take extra caution when dog-proofing for your Maltese; customizing your home environment for a toy breed can require more insight than preparing to bring home a larger dog.

For one thing, it is easy to overlook dangers lurking close to the floor. It is also easy to underestimate the tiny spaces small dogs can squeeze into. Railings along stairways and porches might keep a bigger dog safely contained, but a Maltese can slip effortlessly through them.

Your Maltese can be fatally injured if he falls off a piece of furniture or down a flight of stairs or if he gets accidentally slammed in a door. A swimming pool can be unsafe for a dog of any size, but a small dog can also easily drown in a hot tub, garden pond or accumulated water on top of a covered pool. Small dogs are also more susceptible to toxic reactions from ingesting tiny amounts of substances that normally wouldn't affect a larger dog.

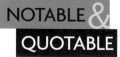

No one ever told Maltese that they were small. They are so willing to please and live up to their names as being alert, loyal, intelligent and sensitive. They have lots of love for their owners, as well as for family and friends.

— breeder Patricia Berge of Butte, Mont.

Your Puppy's Daily Routine

When you first bring your puppy home, she will undoubtedly be the center of attention. But your undivided attention is going to give her very unrealistic ideas about what to expect in her daily life. Sooner or later, she will need to spend time on her own. After all, you can't be with your dog 24/7.

It's much better to let her experience some alone time gradually than to simply lock her behind a gate or inside a crate for a few hours and hope she becomes independent on her own.

Introduce your pup to her designated area the first day she arrives and ensure that she spends some time there each day; incorporate it into her regular schedule. Vary the lengths of your absence. She'll have a much easier time adjusting to this plan if you implement a daily care schedule for her and stick to it.

A consistent daily routine doesn't just facilitates training, it also encourages bonding and teaches your dog to recognize you as her pack leader. Your Maltese will feel more confident and secure knowing when to expect her next food, walk or play session. For instance, a puppy might need to be fed four times and taken to her elimination spot 10 or more times every day.

These activities reinforce the puppy's expectations about her daily routine, which in turn gives her a sense of security about her place in your pack. By adulthood, your dog's needs will alter greatly, and you can revise her schedule substantially. But once your puppy has settled on a consistent routine, make changes gradually. An erratic schedule or sudden, drastic change will confuse her and undermine your training.

CHAPTER
5

HELP WITH

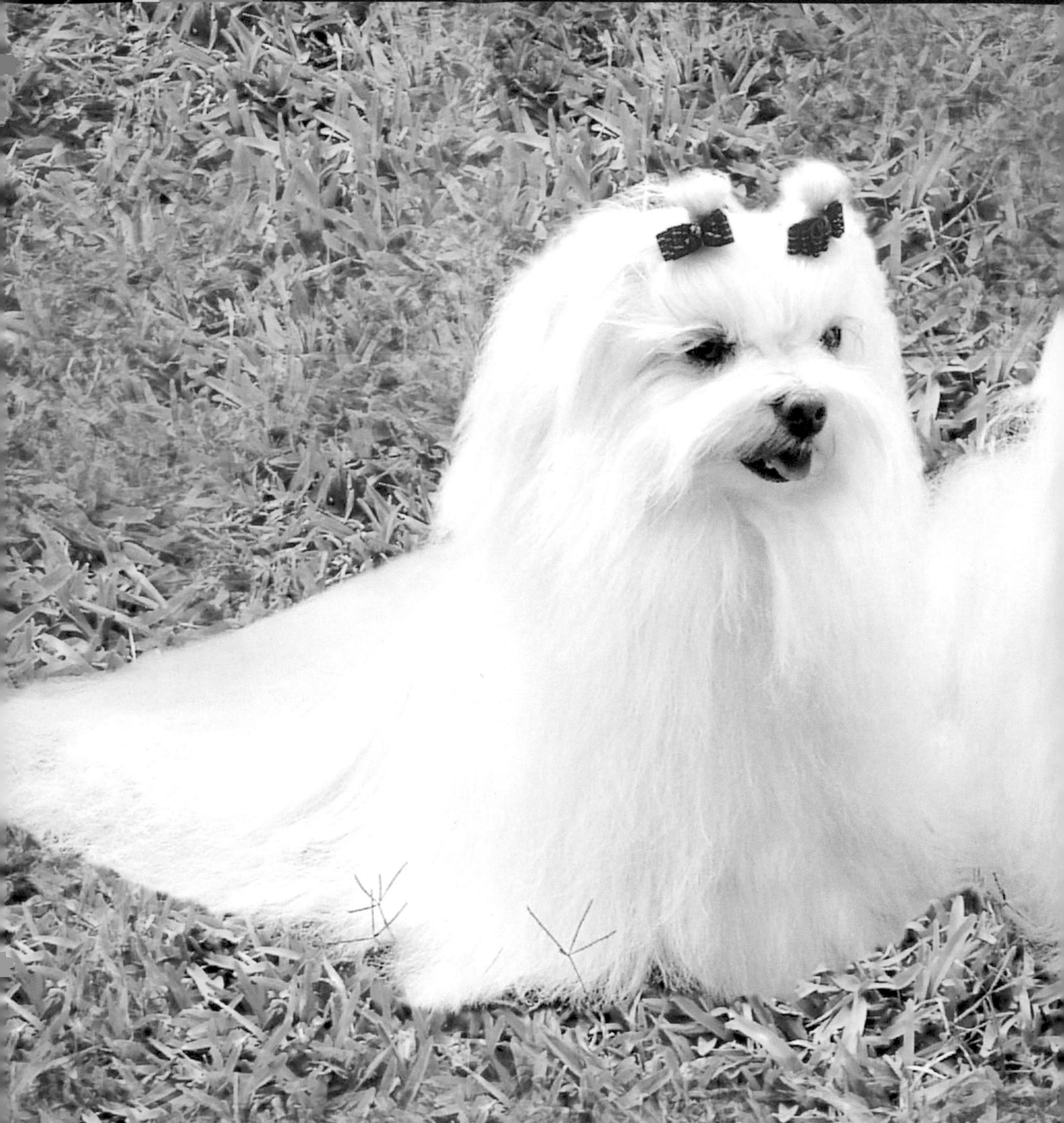

HOUSETRAINING

You will probably want to housetrain your Maltese puppy as soon as you bring him home. But don't skip the first steps in the process: bonding and establishing communication.

Correctly interpreting your puppy's signals is a critical part of successful housetraining. Puppies always provide some clues when they need to eliminate, such as sniffing, circling and whining. All puppies are destined to have their share of accidents before they are reliably housetrained. But learning to read your own puppy's signals and becoming familiar with his body's schedule definitely makes the process easier.

Before you bring your new Maltese home, decide what training method you plan to use. If you plan to train him to use paper or a litter box, stick with that particular routine. Don't alternate from taking him for walks to sending him to your enclosed lawn to expecting him to use indoor papers. Your supervision and consistency are crucial.

Maltese are sensitive, active dogs that enjoy having fun with the people they love. Every waking moment with your Maltese is an opportunity to guide and teach. Proper training and careful socialization will put your pup on the road to success, prevent behavior problems and make life happier for both of you.

it's a
Fact

Encourage your puppy to form a habit of eliminating in one place by taking him to his designated spot at regular intervals all day long. Keep him confined to an area where you can observe him closely throughout the day. Although many Maltese housetrain very quickly, yours may not be completely housetrained until he is about a year old. However long it takes, be prepared to restrict your puppy's home access by using baby gates and exercise pens (also known as X-pens) or by simply shutting the doors to rooms that have wall-to-wall carpeting.

Housetraining isn't an exact science, but consistency plus supervision usually equals success.

Don't make the training process more difficult than it needs to be.

You can probably watch your Maltese's activities if you confine him to one or two rooms. Giving him run of the house will make that impossible. A puppy may not have time to find his way to his papers or through his pet door when he feels the need to go. His elimination spot must be convenient and accessible. If you live in an apartment and are attempting to train a young puppy, you may not want to get dressed, take the elevator to the lobby and walk to the park 15 times a day.

Take your pup to his designated area as soon as he wakes up in the morning, within 10 minutes after he eats, right after play sessions and before retiring for the night. You may need to double this schedule when training a young puppy. You can estimate the number of times he will need to relieve himself each day based on his age. But every dog is different, and you may need to revise this schedule to ensure that he has access to his elimination spot when he regularly needs it.

Puppies less than 3 months old may need to relieve themselves every hour during the day. After three months, they develop better bowel and bladder control, but they usually still need to go at least eight times a day. By 5 months of age, this may reduce to five or six times a day. An adult Maltese should be able to manage fine with four daily potty trips, although senior dogs may need additional opportunities.

An equally important part of the process is to accompany your puppy to make sure that he does what he is there for. This can take a lot of patience. Teaching your puppy a phrase like "go potty" or "do your business" can help him make the association. Rewarding him with praise and a treat when he does it will

Take your dog to her potty spot when you see her giving you signs that she needs to go.

also help to speed up the process. Some trainers recommend using clicker training to help a dog learn this connection.

When you take your dog to his designated elimination spot, wait at least 15 minutes for him to do his business. Don't let your puppy get distracted, which can easily happen. Try not to talk or move around too much until he's done. If you have no success after 15 minutes, don't assume that he didn't need to go. Confine

your pup for half an hour and repeat the routine. Be prepared to do this several times, if necessary. Never act impatient or annoyed. That sort of reaction may inhibit your dog from going at all. Instilling reliable housetraining behavior takes time. Until your puppy is completely trustworthy, you must supervise him constantly and limit his access to your house. Owners often complain that their dogs refuse to eliminate outdoors but then proceed to do

Did You Know?

The desire to scent-mark territory is a basic canine instinct. Neutered and intact males and females, puppies and adults all have the potential to habitually mark their territory. The behavior is characterized by frequently voiding small quantities of urine or feces both indoors and outdoors.

so immediate after they come back into the house. Persistence, praise and supervision should prevent that.

Even if you do everything right, be prepared to cope with some cleanups; scrupulous cleanup is essential to successful housetraining. You may not be able to detect traces of a prior accident, but your dog will. It will provide a constant reminder and potential temptation to use that spot as a bathroom again. If he consistently has accidents in the same place, you may need to restrict his access to that room.

If you catch your puppy having an accident, interrupt him verbally and take him to the right spot. Don't reprimand him after the fact. Instead, your best option is to clean up the mess and remind yourself to supervise more carefully. If you lose your temper or punish your dog for things that happened hours ago, you may soon find yourself coping with behavior problems much worse than housetraining.

Whenever you bring a new dog home, be prepared to spend time introducing him to his housetraining routine. This goes for puppies, adult dogs and dogs that are already trained. It is not unusual for a housetrained dog to relapse when he is introduced to a new environment. He also has no way of adapting his previous habits to your home and schedule unless you provide guidance.

CRATETRAINING

Cratetraining and housetraining are often introduced in tandem. Training your puppy to stay in a crate when you can't supervise him helps speed up the housetraining process immensely, if you do it the right way. Of course, it can also thoroughly undermine the process, if he's habitually confined for long periods of time.

This training method is based on the fact that dogs have a natural aversion to soiling their den areas. As soon as they are old enough to walk, puppies will make an effort to eliminate away from areas where they eat and sleep. But if a puppy is confined to a crate for longer than he can hold out, he will be forced to ignore his natural instinct for cleanliness.

Any dog that is confined to a crate or other small space for long amounts of time before you adopt him will probably be more difficult to housetrain. Once a puppy loses the instinct to keep his den clean, housetraining becomes far more difficult.

If you acquired your Maltese from a breeder, the pup probably had some introduction to staying in a crate at a very young age. This makes the training process much easier. He will understand that a crate is the perfect place for him to curl up and take a peaceful nap.

Begin familiarizing your puppy with his crate as soon as you bring him home; he'll spend time in it in a variety of situations. For safety, he should always stay in his crate during car trips. You may also need the crate during various situations in the home. For instance, crating your dog is a great safety measure if you ever have

How often does a Maltese puppy do her business? A lot! Go to **DogChannel.com/Club-Maltese** and download the typical schedule of a puppy. You can also download a chart that you can fill out to track your dog's elimination timetable, which will help you with housetraining.

JOIN OUR ONLINE
Club Maltese™

NOTABLE & QUOTABLE *On the whole, regular household detergents and cleaners don't help with cleaning up after accidents because the scent always remains, encouraging the puppy or other dogs to reuse the area. There are a couple of spray cleaners available specifically for pet cleanup that contain odor and stain removers. They are excellent for small accidents. There also are products that contain enzymes that work by naturally breaking down the chemicals in the waste and eradicating any odors. These products are effective, though it's important not to try other cleaners before using the enzyme product. Be sure to use these products thoroughly because dogs' noses are many times more sensitive than our own.*

— Kim Barnett, a dog behavior consultant in Stroudsburg, Penn.

Most housetraining problems are due to owner inattention. Let your puppy relieve herself as soon as she wakes up, after she eats and after playtime. Don't give her a chance to have an accident.

workers in your home. A little dog can easily slip through a gate or a door left open. Therefore, it's important that your puppy learn to love his crate rather than just accept it. When done properly, cratetraining reinforces a dog's natural instinct to seek out a safe den.

The cratetraining process is a relatively simple one. Make the crate an inviting place for your dog to spend his time. When first introducing your new puppy to his crate, place a crate pad and a couple of interesting toys inside it. Hiding a treat in the back sometimes helps lure wary pups. Encourage your puppy to enter the crate on his own.

Use a special phrase like "time for bed" or "nap time," and praise him when he enters. If he starts to cry and whine, ignore him. Talking to him or opening the door to pet him will not soothe him into being quiet; it will simply encourage more demands to get out. At first, leave him for just 10 or 15 minutes. Wait until he settles down, then let him out and praise him.

Most puppies accept cratetraining readily, but many owners make it more difficult than it is. If your puppy's cratetraining proves to be difficult, don't encourage unwanted behavior. Whining, crying, barking or digging in the crate is meant to get your attention. Giving in will only prolong the process. Tell him "no, quiet," and don't be tempted to let him out until he complies.

As your Maltese puppy gets older, you can increase the time he spends in the crate. By 4 months old, he should be able to remain crated for three or four hours. Always assume that he will need to relieve himself immediately by this time. By 5 months of age, he should be able to make it through the night without being let out of the crate. However, if he does wake up at 3 a.m. needing to pee, you better get up and take him out. Never let him get into the habit of relieving himself in the crate,

Face it: Accidents will happen. Just realize that you caused the accident and be more diligent in your supervision in the future.

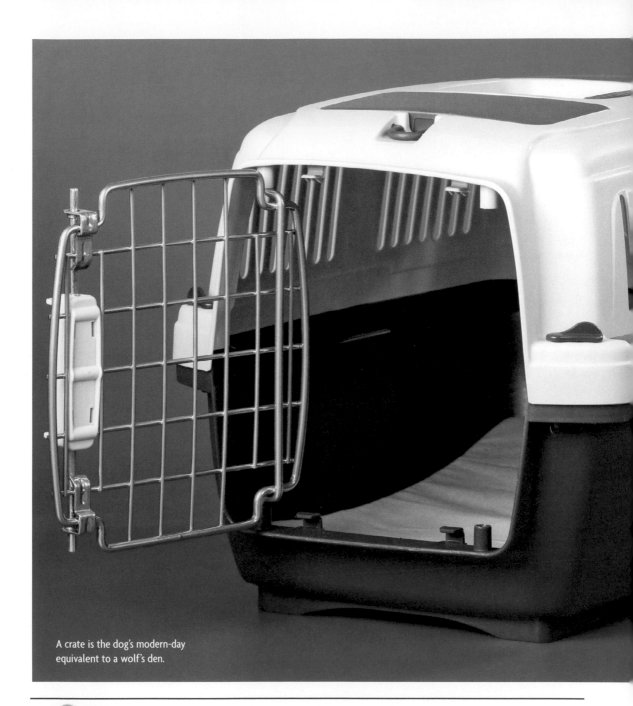

A crate is the dog's modern-day equivalent to a wolf's den.

Having housetraining problems with your Maltese? Ask other Maltese owners for advice and tips, or post your own success story to give other owners encouragement. Log onto **DogChannel.com/Club-Maltese** and click on "Community."

Clean accidents properly. Using an enzyme solution will dramatically reduce the time it takes to housetrain your dog because she won't be drawn back to the same areas. If you need, use a black light to reveal soiled areas that your naked eye can't see. After identifying a soiled area, treat it with the enzyme solution.

regardless of how convenient it may be for you in the moment.

KEEP CLEAN

Here are some other tips for cleaning potty accidents:

◆ Never use ammonia for cleaning an accident. Urine contains ammonia, so the chemical will keep attracting your dog to the spot. Bleach is a better cleaner, but be sure to rinse well in any areas that you use it. Also, be sure to use color-safe bleach where appropriate.

◆ White vinegar is a good odor remover, if you don't have any professional cleaners on hand; use 1/4 cup to 1 quart of water.

◆ Salt will absorb fresh urine and remove some of the scent.

◆ In a pinch, rubbing the area with a dryer sheet can remove some of the odor.

◆ Baking soda rubbed into a urine stain can remove some of the odor.

◆ If the urine scent on your wooden floor won't come out, consider painting or sealing it.

◆ A peroxide-and-water solution will help get rid of carpet stains. Experiment with various strengths of solution.

◆ White toothpaste can get some tough stains out of carpets.

◆ If the stains are really bad, your best bet is to call a professional carpet cleaner.

Make sure to take your puppy to the same potty spot each time. Eventually, she'll know that it's her "bathroom."

Actions speak louder than words. When we're anxious about something, the dog will be anxious, too. Anticipate the behavior and meet it head on with reassurance and a calm, soothing voice. — breeder/trainer Brenda Morris of Las Vegas, Nev.

Housetraining Tip List

1 Decide where you want your dog to eliminate. This could be anywhere from a quiet place outdoors to a convenient indoor litter box. Training methods are basically the same for both, and both have their advantages and disadvantages. If you train your dog to go outdoors you won't have to bother with the hassle of changing litter, but nasty weather can make many Maltese choose to go to the bathroom indoors instead of outside.

Training your Maltese to use a litter box can give your dog independence to eliminate on her own as needed, and it frees you up from having to take her outside all throughout the day. Some owners decide to take their dogs to outdoor potty areas but have them use litter boxes when the weather is bad or when they're not home.

Litter boxes are often the best solution for high-rise apartment dwellers, but the devices can also help keep rural pet owners' Maltese safe from coyotes, eagles and other predators that would consider the bite-size dogs as tasty snacks. Regardless of what you choose, until your dog is reliably housetrained, don't leave your pup unsupervised in or out of your home.

2 If the approved potty area becomes too soiled, your pup will seek cleaner places to eliminate. Scoop the potty area daily, leaving one "reminder" poop for your pup while she's still learning.

3 Keep potty trips for business only, not for play. Take your dog to the designated spot, calmly tell her to "go potty" (or use another preferred phrase) and then wait. If she needs to eliminate, she will go within a few minutes. Praise calmly, then wait a little longer in case she's not done.

4 To help you anticipate potty breaks, keep a chart noting when and where your Maltese eliminates. Regularly timed meals make for more predictable elimination, so feed on a schedule instead of leaving food out all the time.

5 Hang a bell from your doorknob at dog-nose height. Each time you take your Maltese out to go potty, ring the bell. Most dogs quickly connect the bell ringing with the door opening, and they soon try it themselves. Eventually, your dog will be able to alert you to when she needs to go out.

6 Dogs naturally return to re-soil where they've eliminated, so thoroughly clean up any accidents and leave the scent in any areas you want your dog to return to.

7 If you catch your Maltese going potty in the wrong place, interrupt her verbally but don't scold her. Gently carry her to her approved area, let her finish, then praise. If you're too late to interrupt the accident in progress, scoop the poop or blot the pee with a paper towel, then take the waste and your Maltese (gently!) to the proper potty area. Place the poop or wipe the urine there, and praise your pup if she sniffs or goes potty in the designated area.

8 Don't punish your puppy's potty mistakes. Punishment can cause dogs to start hiding poop and pee in dark corners or behind furniture — or even eating it to destroy the evidence.

9 The best way to prevent male Maltese from urine marking indoors is to neuter them while they are young (before they start lifting their legs to urinate; consult your veterinarian for the best age to schedule the surgery). If your male marks indoors, a belly-band "diaper" may solve the problem. The device fastens with Velcro around the dog's waist and absorbs urine as he tries to mark. Most dogs notice their marking attempts backfiring immediately and give up the habit; meanwhile, your house stays clean. You can buy belly bands at a pet-supply store or make one from a sock with a sanitary pad tucked inside.

10 If you think your Maltese's housetraining is taking an unusually long amount of time, consult your veterinarian to rule out health problems. Slow housetraining or lapses in training can signal bladder or bowel problems. A dog that seems stubborn may actually be ill.

HANDS

Choosing a veterinarian for your Maltese is a critical part of his healthcare. Don't make a haphazard selection or put it off until he becomes ill. The easiest way to find a vet is by asking your puppy's breeder or your dog-owning friends and neighbors for their suggestions. Accessibility is an important consideration to keep in mind when you're deciding on a vet. You should be able to schedule same-day appointments to see your veterinarian and reach him or her after hours if needed. And the vet should provide referrals to a nearby emergency clinic if he or she doesn't offer emergency care.

Does the vet have a good reputation among toy-breed owners? Some vets aren't experienced treating small dogs. The vet must consider the breeds' metabolic differences when administering anesthesia and vaccinations and while calibrating drug dosages. A particular drug regimen or procedure may be safe for larger dogs but dangerous for Maltese.

Will you be able to see the same vet at each appointment? This isn't always an option at a large clinic, which you may consider to be a disadvantage. If you go to the same veterinarian each visit, he or she will become familiar with your dog's health history, and both you and your dog will

have the opportunity to become comfortable with the veterinarian. Since you're the one ultimately responsible for your dog's health decisions, make sure you feel comfortable asking your vet any health-related questions and discussing the associated costs in advance of various procedures.

Cost may not be your main priority when making health-related decisions for your Maltese, but you should feel confident about the vet's recommendations. The most costly option may not always be the best one for your dog, and you should be able to trust your vet to provide you the best — not just the most expensive — medical advice. Diagnostic testing doesn't always provide a clear-cut identification of a problem. In that

The most common causes of coughing and sneezing in puppies are the result of viral or bacterial upper-respiratory tract infections. Other common causes of coughing and sneezing in dogs include a dry environment, a foreign body in the nose (such as a plant part), and irritation from dust or pollen. If your pup is coughing or sneezing, keep her warm and well fed, avoid stress and interaction with other animals, and watch for worsening of the symptoms, which will warrant a vet visit.

it's a Fact

case, find a vet who favors exploring conservative treatment options first.

HEALTH CHECK

Schedule a routine checkup for your Maltese within two or three days of bringing him home to confirm that he is in good health. Your vet will examine his heart, eyes, ears, throat, mouth, gums and teeth, and he'll also check your pup's respiration, weight, body temperature, and skin and coat conditions.

Your vet may ask you to bring a fecal sample to check for intestinal parasites. Puppies don't always have worms, and deworming medication should never be administered unless it's needed. The vet may also recommend starting your Maltese on a heartworm preventive depending on the season and climate. Heartworm has become a year-round problem in some parts of the country. In other places, dogs only need preventives during the mosquito season. Either way, the vet will need to test your Maltese's blood to ensure that he does not have heartworms before starting him on a preventive. Your pup may also need one or more vaccinations.

ANNUAL HEALTH EXAM

Most likely, your Maltese will enjoy years of uninterrupted good health. Annual health exams will ensure that he stays healthy. Depending on your dog's age and condition, your vet may focus on different aspects of the general exam. For instance, your vet may recommend blood testing, urinalysis or X-rays for senior dogs or as a follow up to any unusual findings. Your dog will also need yearly fecal testing to detect internal parasites. Symptoms are not always immediately obvious, but they will become worse over time if left untreated and undetected. Your pup's annual

When you bring home a new dog, always take her to your vet right away for an initial checkup.

vet visit shouldn't automatically include vaccinations or a full anesthesia dental cleaning. These treatments aren't without risk, so make sure they are necessary before agreeing to them.

Your vet may recommend twice-yearly health exams if your Maltese is more than 7 years old. Many age-related problems respond well to early treatment, and your vet can watch for these issues more easily if you bring your dog in for checkups more frequently. Small bumps and growths can be biopsied to possibly identify early stages of cancer. Early detection and biopsy analysis are vital in determining the best course of treatment.

PREVENTIVE HEALTH CARE

Your veterinarian will play a central role in keeping your Maltese healthy, but your own sensible preventive care is equally important. It's up to you to watch for subtle changes in your dog's health and behavior that would merit a visit to the vet. Obviously, you'll need to treat serious injuries or sudden illnesses immediately, but many ailments are preceded by subtle changes. Early detection and treatment can often limit their severity. Get in the habit of giving your Maltese a quick health check every day. Skin irritations; slight lameness; unusual lumps or swelling; or changes in his eating, drinking or elimination habits may not require an immediate consultation with your vet. But if they persist for a couple of days, find out what's going on.

DIET AND EXERCISE

A healthy diet and adequate exercise are also important. Make small modifications in your dog's diet to keep him at his ideal weight, rather than waiting until the situation calls for drastic measures. Every dog needs regular daily exercise, even a tiny Maltese. Two 15-minute exercise sessions per day will keep him in good mental and physical condition. It's also good for *your* physical well-being!

Outdoor exercise is the best choice, but it may not be possible in cold or rainy weather. In that case, a couple of play sessions will provide an equally good workout. Don't just leave your Maltese in the backyard by himself, though; Maltese are not physically or mentally equipped to spend large amounts of time outdoors alone. Your dog will get bored and lonely, and his coat does not provide adequate protection from the elements. The Maltese's single-layered silky coat is not designed to insulate him from cold, heat, dampness or sunlight.

Use common sense when exercising your Maltese outdoors in colder weather. If it's cold enough for you to wear a coat, put one on your dog, too. Even that won't protect him for extended periods of time, though. Small dogs lose body heat comparatively faster than large dogs. Protect your Maltese's feet from cold, ice and chemical ice-removers on sidewalks. Keep the hair on his footpads trimmed short to prevent ice from adhering, and coat his pads with paw wax for added protection. Some dogs even accept wearing boots, but many don't. After a walk, always check your dog's feet for injuries.

Perhaps you have more ambitious plans in mind for your Maltese beyond walking in the park and playing leisurely games of tug of war. In that case, common-sense precautions are essential. During major growth periods, minimize any activities that can cause bone and joint stress. Maltese should not begin any serious exercise regimens before reaching 8 months of age. Before you start, have your vet examine your dog to make sure he is in good health.

Gradual conditioning is essential for anyone embarking on a sports program — human or canine. Even if your dog is keen to keep going, it is your responsibility to make sure he does not overexert himself. Slowly work toward your exercise goals and occasionally vary the routine. This not only keeps him from getting bored, but it also ensures that all muscle groups get a workout. Above all, always remain mindful of your dog's safety. This includes preventing athletic injuries and being observant of environmental factors that could pose dangers.

DENTAL CARE

Routine dental care isn't just cosmetic. Although dogs don't develop cavities, they are prone to equally devastating problems if their oral health is neglected. Plaque (sticky debris made up of proteins and food particles) can be easily removed when it is first deposited on the teeth.

If left untreated, however, it will harden into a bacteria-laden substance that will work its way under the gums and cause periodontal disease. At this stage, it causes bad breath and inflamed, receding, bleeding gums. The teeth will loosen as the roots become damaged by infection.

At this point, an owner usually will notice that his or her dog has extremely bad breath or is not eating. More serious implications of poor oral heath are less obvious. Periodontal disease can spread bacteria throughout the bloodstream, damaging major organs. Infected and abscessed teeth can also lead to bone infection or bone loss in the lower jaw. For tiny dogs, this is extremely dangerous. Their already fragile jaw bones can easily fracture, and repairing infected or eroded bone may not be possible.

If your Maltese is suffering from periodontal disease, he will need dental cleaning and possible extractions under full anesthesia, followed by antibiotic therapy. It is painful, costly and unavoidable at this point, but all treatments are preventable with regular dental hygiene.

Do your dog a favor and brush his teeth regularly. This becomes more important as he gets older, but it is difficult to introduce an adult dog to a dental routine. Teach your puppy to accept daily brushing even though his teeth may look clean. It will save you both a lot of grief later in life. Daily brushing is the best way to remove plaque before it hardens into tartar. You can also try giving your dog daily applications of a cleaning gel containing zinc ascorbate to control tartar formation on his teeth. Crunchy foods and safe dental chews can also keep tartar from accumulating.

In recent years, dental chews have become a popular way to prevent tartar buildup. Dogs love them, and their abrasive textures scrape plaque from the teeth. However, vets and manufacturers warn to only give your dog the treats under your supervision. Aggressive chewing can lead to fractured teeth, and ingesting pieces of these chews can cause respiratory or gastrointestinal obstruction.

Chews are typically designed as toys rather than as food items. They are not manufactured to be digestible, although many dogs can and will tear off small pieces and swallow them. Since chew treats are labeled as toys, they do not fall under regulatory control for food products, and manufacturers are not liable for health and safety concerns. Potential risks vary depending on the type of chew.

Cured rawhide is digestible, but it breaks down very slowly and can induce severe gastric irritation or partial gut obstruction in the process. Some dental chews (sometimes labeled as "healthy edibles") break into large chunks when chewed, which poses a greater risk of lodging in the esophagus or windpipe.

Hard plastic chews are generally regarded as safest because they're difficult — but not impossible — for most dogs to dismantle. Needless to say, they are indigestible. But keep in mind that flavored versions are more edibly enticing. If your dog does manage to swallow part of one, it can cause an obstruction, and the plastic debris won't show up on an X-ray. Softer plastic chews may contain a significant PVC (polyvinyl chloride) content. These chemical compounds are banned from use in children's plastic toys but not for dogs.

When selecting chews for your Maltese, be sure they are manufactured in the United States and that they contain safe ingredients. If you aren't sure which size to get, larger is safer than smaller, especially if you have multiple dogs. One Maltese may not be capable of severely crushing a hard chew, but don't underestimate the damage that two or three dogs can manage together. Discard chew toys when they show signs of wear

Make sure your Maltese's teeth stay as white as his coat.

Just like with infants, puppies need a series of vaccinations to ensure that they stay healthy during their first year of life. Download a vaccination chart from **DogChannel.com/Club-Maltese** that you can fill out for your dog.

or become excessively dirty. Despite manufacturer claims, there is no such thing as an indestructible chew. They also harbor germs and can spread disease from one dog to another.

LESS IS MORE

Thanks to recent advances in research, we are more aware of immune-mediated disorders. Like humans, some dogs are genetically susceptible but never develop immune disorders because they aren't exposed to situations that trigger them.

There are numerous potential triggers, which dogs are exposed to more today than ever before. Injury, exhaustion, and physical or mental stress definitely compromises a dog's immune function. Toxic exposure poses major risks, some of which are not obvious, such as synthetic food additives, cleaning agents, second-hand cigarette smoke and pesticides.

Recent illness, internal or external parasites and excessive use of antibiotics, immunosuppressive drugs or corticosteroid vaccinations can also compromise a dog's immune system functions. These things won't cause allergies, but they will make a dog more susceptible.

ALLERGIES

Some Maltese are allergy prone, due to a combination of genetic predisposition, environmental exposure and weakened immune systems. Environmental allergies often run in families. They can be chronic or seasonal and often become worse with age. Elderly dogs tend to develop allergic reactions more frequently, as their immune functions become less efficient.

A susceptible dog can become allergic to just about anything: from prescription and nonprescription drugs and vaccinations to foods or food additives, household cleaning agents, insecticides, grooming products, grass, weeds, pollen, dust, mold, etc. The list is endless. But the dog must have had prior exposure to the allergen in order to mount a reaction. Usually, the dog's initial exposure occurs during puppyhood, but dogs younger than 6 months old rarely develop allergies.

Allergens can enter a dog's system by inhalation, ingestion or through the skin. After exposure to the allergy-causing substance, the dog's immune system launches an attack by releasing chemical compounds, most notably histamines, into the bloodstream. This is what produces the reaction. Most commonly, allergic reactions are characterized by intense itching and inflammation, especially around the ears, feet and tail. Dogs may also develop eye irritation, persistent coughs or bronchitis.

Flea bites are the most common allergy culprit. The proteins in flea saliva will cause severe itching and inflammation. The dog's uncontrollable licking and scratching leads to deep secondary bacterial and fungal infections. Topical or oral cortisone can provide temporarily relief, but the reaction will recur if fleas bite again or if you stop administering the medication.

Food allergies can cause reactions ranging from vomiting, diarrhea and abdominal cramps to skin irritations or respiratory distress. It is possible for a dog to develop an allergic reaction to a food that he has eaten regularly in the past. Because symptoms are variable and often respond temporarily to treatments, food allergies can be difficult to diagnose.

Your vet may recommend blood tests, skin tests or an elimination diet to discover which substances your dog is allergic to. Treatment can be as simple as removing the allergens from the environment. If that is not possible, however, antihistamine or hyposensitization vaccines can stimulate a dog's immunity to the allergic substance and often alleviates symptoms for many dogs. If all else fails, ask your vet for recommendations on steroid treatments, topical and oral antibiotics, or cortisone ointments to help control itching and inflammation.

Some allergic reactions can be fatal. Anaphylactic shock most commonly occurs in response to a drug, vaccination or insect sting. The dog will develop severe respiratory distress, pale gums and a rapid drop in blood pressure within 30 minutes of exposure. This is a life-threatening emergency that requires immediate medical attention.

Dogs can get seasonal or chronic allergies, too.

Did You Know?

Puppies are usually born without teeth. Between 3 and 6 weeks of age, pups get their deciduous (or baby) teeth. Then, between 3 and 7 months of age, puppies begin to shed their baby teeth as the adult teeth grow in. At least, that's what is supposed to happen. Sometimes, the baby teeth still remain, even as the adult teeth grow in, meaning two teeth occupy the same socket at the same time. There is only one treatment: extraction of the retained deciduous tooth. When done in a timely fashion, the adult teeth will grow in normally and no permanent damage will occur. If you wait to treat it, the crowding could cause dental misalignment.

VACCINATIONS

The immunity puppies receive from their mothers protects them for 5 to 12 weeks. Vaccinations are not effective until a puppy's maternal immunity has declined, and this occurs at a variable rate.

When that happens, the puppy will need a series of vaccinations, although the exact components of these vaccinations can vary. American Animal Hospital Association guidelines recommend that all puppies receive vaccinations for distemper, hepatitis (adenovirus), parainfluenza, and parvovirus. These are all usually given as one combined vaccination. Some versions of the combination shot also contain ingredients to protect the dog from additional diseases, which your puppy may not need.

Maltese breeders generally avoid giving the leptospirosis vaccine to puppies because it is most often implicated in vaccine reactions. After your puppy is vaccinated, his immunity to disease develops gradually. Occasionally, immunity doesn't occur until the third vaccination. Therefore, it is important to keep your puppy isolated from other dogs until he's completed all his shots.

Annual revaccination might not be necessary for every dog. Some Maltese owners prefer to have their dogs' antibody titer levels tested to determine when booster shots are needed. Your vet can conduct this blood test annually as part of your dog's regular checkup.

The benefits of the protection your dog will receive against highly contagious and potentially fatal illnesses far outweigh the risks associated with administering the vaccines. Some of these diseases are treatable; most are not. Even in cases when dogs recover, many suffer permanent side effects such as neurological impairment or permanent secondary organ damage. Your dog doesn't necessarily need to have direct contact with an infected dog in order to contract one of these diseases. The modes of transmission can vary, and some types of bacteria can remain functional in the environment for months.

Vaccines are classified as "core" and "noncore." Core vaccines are essential; noncore components are optional. Their value depends on your dog's environment and lifestyle. Ask your vet for advice when deciding which are necessary for your Maltese.

CORE VACCINES

Distemper: Distemper is a highly contagious viral disease. For centuries, it was the most dreaded canine killer. All dogs are susceptible to it, and it is present in all dog populations. The symptoms can appear one to three weeks after exposure and include depression, loss of appetite, vomiting, diarrhea, nasal and ocular discharge,

Did You Know? **Female dogs are spayed by removing their reproductive organs, and male dogs are neutered by removing their testicles.** The spay surgery (or ovariohysterectomy, as your veterinarian may refer to it) is the most commonly performed surgery on companion animals in the United States. Removal of the testicles (neutering) is the most common form of sterilization in male dogs in the United States. In both cases, the operation is performed while the pup is anesthetized. The vast majority of dogs recover quickly, without any complications from anesthesia or surgery.

seizures and paralysis. Bronchitis, pneumonia and neurological damage are common secondary complications. Treatment consists of supportive care, such as keeping the dog well hydrated, warm and nourished in order to fight off the infection. For some diseases, it also includes treating secondary complications, such as eye infections.

Parvovirus: Canine parvovirus is highly contagious; it killed thousands of dogs before a vaccine became available in the 1970s. It is easily spread to dogs by humans carrying the virus on their hands, shoes or clothing. Symptoms of sudden and severe vomiting, bloody diarrhea, dehydration and shock appear two to seven days after exposure. Dogs of all ages are susceptible, but it is most often fatal in puppies. Treatment consists of supportive care.

Adenovirus: Infectious canine vadenovirus (hepatitis) is highly contagious, contracted by direct or indirect contact. Symptoms include conjunctivitis, tonsillitis, loss of appetite, jaundice and abdominal tenderness. Recovered animals often suffer chronic liver or kidney damage.

Rabies: Rabies is carried and spread through the saliva of infected individuals. The virus attacks the central nervous system. Symptoms include disorientation, headache, nervousness, drooling, seizures and hallucinations. Once major symptoms appear, rabies is invariably fatal. Rabies vaccinations have been required for all dogs in the United States since the 1950s.

NONCORE VACCINES

Leptospirosis bacterium: Spread by wildlife or contact with infected soil or vegetation, leptospirosis bacterium can live in damp soil or standing water for many months and is transmissible from dogs to humans. Symptoms appear two to four weeks after exposure and include fever, muscle pain, lack of appetite, extreme thirst,

Take your Maltese for regular vet checkups to keep an eye out for common breed health problems.

---

jaundice and leg swelling. Prognosis is poor because infection can lead to irreversible liver or kidney damage. Maltese breeders don't recommend giving leptospirosis vaccinations because it is associated with many vaccine reactions. If you live in a high-risk area, try to minimize your dog's exposure to possible sources of infection. Some strains are transmitted by wildlife, others are transmitted by livestock. Ponds, puddles and damp ground can all harbor live bacteria. The urine of infected dogs is another major source of contagion.

Bordetella: Kennel cough is a highly contagious airborne disease, similar to whooping cough in humans. The incubation period can range from 12 to 14 days. Most adult dogs recover without treatment. Elderly or debilitated dogs or puppies may need antibiotics to prevent serious secondary infection or pneumonia. Nasal vaccines are considered safer and more reliable.

Lyme disease: Lyme disease is the first of several tick-borne diseases identified in the United States. Symptoms can vary from mild to severe and may include limping, joint pain, fever, loss of appetite and swollen lymph nodes. If you find a tick on your Maltese, remove it with tweezers, place it in a sealed container and take it to your vet for analyzation. Prompt treatment is crucial. Vaccination against Lyme disease is sometimes recommended for dogs that live in high-risk areas, but its safety and effectiveness remains controversial.

VACCINE REACTIONS

Adverse reactions to certain vaccine components are known to be greater in certain breeds or families within some breeds. Unless the dog is already predisposed to an allergic reaction to a vaccine's component, vaccination doesn't cause an allergy; however, vaccination can trigger reactions in a susceptible dog, and excessive vaccinations make this possibility more likely. Both killed and modified live vaccines can trigger allergic reactions. They can occur any time from immediately after vaccination to several weeks or months later. Symptoms can range from fever, lethargy, lack of appetite or facial swelling to potentially fatal reactions including shock, liver failure or injection-site sarcomas.

Your breeder may recommend avoiding certain vaccine components if your Maltese has a familial sensitivity. Use common sense when having your Maltese vaccinated. Illness and stress will affect his immune system's ability to effectively respond to a vaccination. Don't take your dog in for a vaccination right before a stressful event, such as going on a trip or being boarded at a kennel. Definitely don't have him vaccinated shortly before or after surgery, when he's recovering from an illness or during any treatments using immunosuppressive drugs. At best, the drugs will render the vaccines ineffective, but in some cases, vaccination can actually cause a dog to develop the disease rather than induce protection against it.

INTERNAL PARASITES AND DEWORMING

Dogs can contract worms, hookworms and tapeworms just about anywhere. Have your vet check for parasites every year as part of your dog's annual health exam. The most common symptoms are lethargy, diarrhea, vomiting, failure to gain weight and a pot-bellied appearance. Severe cases can lead to anemia and respiratory complications.

If necessary, your vet will prescribe a safe, appropriate dewormer. Don't attempt to treat your dog with over-the-counter parasite remedies, and never administer a

Getting rid of fleas means cleaning not just your dog, but also his bed, crate and the entire home.

combination of topical or oral parasite medications to your Maltese. These are toxic substances; giving inappropriate doses or mixing them can cause fatal reactions in small dogs.

Deworming will only be a temporary solution unless you discover the source of the problem and prevent recurrence. Your dog can contract worms from contaminated soil or water, contact with wild or stray animals, or low-level flea infestations. Both roundworms and hookworms can be transmitted to humans. As a precaution, you should always wash your hands after handling or petting dogs you aren't familiar with.

EXTERNAL PARASITES

Fleas: Flea prevention is far easier than flea eradication. One or two fleas are easy to overlook, but a minor problem can turn very serious before you become aware of it. Get in the habit of checking your Maltese for signs of fleas whenever you groom him. The first signs of the problem to keep an eye out for are usually persistent scratching and gritty, black flea dirt.

You can use topical applications to keep the fleas off your Maltese, but effective flea control must include treating the environment to eradicate fleas and eggs from your bedding, furniture, rugs and grass. If you

NOTABLE & QUOTABLE

It's now been proven that injured animals are usually restless and unable to lie still. If you offer them pain relief, they will rest better, be in less pain and be at less risk of tearing out an incision. If you're shopping for a veterinarian and you run across one who doesn't believe in pain relief for a routine surgery, then knock on the next door until you find somebody who understands the need for it.

— Christine Wilford, D.V.M., of Seattle, Wash.

live in an area where fleas are a perpetual problem, your vet can help you design a safe flea-control program. If possible, stick with natural flea-control products, but they may not be as effective if you are dealing with a serious problem. Fleas are now immune to most of them.

Ticks: If you live in a tick-prone region, incorporate tick inspections into your dog's daily grooming routine. If you find one, pull it off with tweezers or hemostatic scissors; don't use kerosene, gasoline or a lit match. Tick-borne diseases (including Lyme disease, Rocky Mountain spotted fever and ehrlichiosis) have spread to several regions of the United States.

If you live in a region where any of these diseases are prevalent and you find a tick on your Maltese, take him to your vet for testing immediately. Prompt treatment can make a big difference in the outcome of your pet's health.

Heartworm: Heartworm has become prevalent in much of the United States, but year-round protection isn't always required. Your Maltese must have a blood test before starting on a preventive. You can administer new medications monthly or even biannually. Many preventives also protect against intestinal parasites.

The disease is spread by mosquitoes carrying heartworm larvae. Once a dog is bitten by an infected mosquito, the larvae enter the bloodstream and lodge in the heart. Symptoms of heartworm infestation include lethargy, coughing, anemia and eventual heart failure. Even if a dog doesn't show obvious symptoms, heartworm will weaken his health and make him more susceptible to other diseases.

Spaying a female dog or neutering a male dog has more benefits than just avoiding unwanted puppies. An altered dog will behave better, will be easier to housetrain or obedience train, and will not be as susceptible to some diseases.

If you don't plan to show your Maltese, it is best to have him or her fixed. Consult your breeder about the best age to do the procedure. Puppies are usually spayed or neutered around 5 or 6 months of age, but this timeframe is based more out of convention than actual research on the best age for the procedure. Very small dogs may benefit from waiting until they are larger, stronger and have had an opportunity to benefit from hormonal changes associated with adolescence.

Fixing your dog may be a routine procedure, but it is still a major surgery that requires full anesthesia. It is not risk-free. Risks can be minimized by using anesthesia that is considered safest for toy breeds, such as a gas anesthetic like isoflurane or sevolurane. The gas is administered into the dog's lungs through an endotracheal tube. The dosage can be adjusted during surgery, and the dog will awaken quickly after it is stopped.

Your Maltese must not have any food or water for eight hours before surgery. The vet will shave and scrub the site of the incision with antiseptic soap to minimize infection risk.

After surgery, the vet will place your dog in a recovery room until he or she awakens. Most dogs are on their feet and behaving normally within a few hours of surgery, but sometimes a vet may want to keep a dog for observation overnight.

Typically, the vet will send your dog home with medication to minimize post-surgical pain and aid in a speedy recovery. Restrict your Maltese's activities for a few days and watch to make sure he or she doesn't lick and pick at the incision site. Otherwise, your pup may need to wear an Elizabethan collar until the healing's complete.

I t's a fact of nature that all animals, including humans, carry certain defective genes that can develop into a full-blown hereditary disease early or late in life. One dog breed can have genetic tendencies toward certain breed-specific illnesses that another might not. The same goes for the Maltese.

In the Maltese breed, the genetic problems that pose some concern are listed in this chapter. Although only a small percentage of Maltese will ever develop any of these problems, the American Maltese Association and conscientious breeders are taking steps to further reduce those odds; they encourage and employ sound breeding practices and support veterinary research into improved diagnostics, better treatments and genetic testing to screen against defective genes in breeding candidates. Here is a closer look at the diseases your Maltese hopefully will never encounter. (Always consult your vet in order to properly care for your Maltese when he is ill.)

HEMORRHAGIC GASTROENTERITIS

HGE is characterized by a sudden bout of severe vomiting and bloody diarrhea with no obvious cause. It is more common in toy breeds, and some dogs are at a high risk of repeated bouts of the problem.

Symptoms such as vomiting, lethargy and anorexia can appear two to 10 days after exposure. Loose stool will quickly progress to watery and bloody diarrhea. Without prompt treatment, the severity of the symptoms can quickly lead to dehydration and shock. A vet can administer an IV to restore fluid balance. In some cases, he or she may also give the dog plasma to correct protein loss, antibiotics to combat infection or cortisone to counteract shock. If your Maltese has repeated episodes of HGE, your vet can examine a culture to determine the bacteria causing the infection. Some vets also recommend giving an over-the-counter antacid daily as a preventive.

DIGESTIVE UPSETS

You can treat minor cases of vomiting and diarrhea at home. Common causes include overeating, gulping water or food too fast, sudden dietary changes, travel sickness and ingesting indigestible substances. Dogs are natural scavengers, and their gastrointestinal tracts are designed to quickly expel unfortunate dietary choices.

If your dog seems fine otherwise and vomits only once or twice, administer an over-the-counter remedy to help settle his stomach.

Withhold water for a couple of hours until his stomach settles. Otherwise, he might immediately regurgitate it, causing additional fluid loss. Once his stomach settles, give him small, frequent drinks of water frequently to prevent dehydration. Do not allow him to gulp an entire bowl of water. Repeated drinking and vomiting can cause dehydration and shock. If your pup is very thirsty, give him ice cubes to lick or a pediatric glucose drink. You can mix a homemade version of this from:

- 1 quart water
- 1 tablespoon sugar
- 1 teaspoon table salt

When the vomiting subsides, withhold food for at least 12 hours and offer your dog bland food. Don't force him to eat. Give small portions of boiled chicken or cooked hamburger and rice. Even if he eats it all and wants more, wait until you are certain his stomach can handle it. Don't let him overeat or gulp his food. Gradually resume feeding his normal diet over a period of three days.

NOTABLE & QUOTABLE

My 11-year-old Maltese runs up and down the stairs like a puppy so she can keep up with what's happening all over the house. Well-bred Maltese are basically healthy dogs, with few of the severe health issues found in many other breeds. Many Maltese live well into their teens, with only yearly veterinarian visits for shots and teeth cleaning. — Linda Lamoureux from Anchorage, Alaska, a Maltese breeder and former Health Committee Chairperson for the American Maltese Association

Any time a young puppy vomits, be prepared to take action. Most vomiting in pups is not innocuous. Gastrointestinal parasites, canine parvovirus, overheating (the early stages of a heatstroke), or another object lodged in the intestines or stomach all lead to vomiting. Seek veterinary care immediately.

Take your Maltese to the vet immediately if he has sever or repeated bouts of vomiting or diarrhea lasting longer than a day or related symptoms such as pain, fever, choking or gagging, weakness, diarrhea, or blood in his vomit or stool. This may indicate an infectious disease, a systemic disorder such as kidney failure or pancreatitis, a heavy infestation of intestinal parasites or a potential poisoning.

PATELLAR LUXATION

Patellar luxation (a dislocated kneecap) is one of the most common orthopedic disorders affecting small dogs. The kneecap is normally anchored in place by strong ligaments resting in grooves on the bone's surface. If it dislocates, it can rotate inward (medial dislocation) or in a less commonly outward position (lateral dislocation).

Shallow or nonexistent grooves are the most common cause, but it can also happen as a result of loose ligaments in the knee joint, weak attachments holding the kneecap in place, an abnormal curvature of the thigh bone, or injury. Most often, one leg is affected, but 25 percent of cases involve both legs.

The main symptom is intermittent lameness without any pain. A dog won't be able to fully extend his leg when his kneecap dislocates. He'll usually hop or skip for a few steps until it pops back into position, which may be accompanied by a clearly audible click. In more serious cases, a dog won't be able to bear weight on his affected leg, and he'll frequently shift his weight to relieve the discomfort. Your vet will be able to diagnose this during a routine exam. X-rays aren't necessary, except to determine the extent of the defect in severe cases.

Secondary arthritis is a common secondary complication. Mildly affected older dogs can suffer sudden lameness after minor trauma due to a breakdown of the joint and tissue after years of continual stress on the weakened joint. This may even occur in both legs simultaneously, rendering the dog suddenly unable to stand after some minor exertion, like jumping off a couch. In the most severe cases, the dog will be unable to extend his leg or bear any weight on it.

Your vet might recommend surgical correction depending on the dog's general health and the extent of joint degeneration. Luxations (joint dislocations) caused by injury generally do not respond well to surgical correction.

LEGG-CALVE-PERTHES DISEASE

Legg-Calve-Perthes disease is most often seen in dogs that weigh less than 25 pounds, such as Maltese. Symptoms usually appear between the ages of 4 and 12 months, with 7 months being the most common age of onset. It is a genetically based condition that causes insufficient blood supply to the ball of the hip joint. As the blood supply diminishes, the bone degenerates and muscle wastes away; a dog's intermittent limping will become more pronounced.

LCP usually occurs only in one hip, but 10 to 15 percent of dogs with LCP are affected in both hips. The first symptom most owners notice is an occasional limp, with no pain. X-rays can confirm the problem, revealing increased space within the joint.

If the disease isn't advanced, vets often recommend to completely confine affected dog to their crates for four to six months. If successful, confinement allows the femoral head to heal sufficiently and permits unrestricted weight-bearing on the joint. Try this conservative form of treatment for at least one month. If there is no improvement or the condition is advanced at the time of diagnosis, your dog may need surgical repair. The surgery involves removing the damaged joint and allowing the hip to form a false joint. Without treatment, at this stage, the dog would suffer muscular atrophy, severe arthritis and permanent disability. After surgery, the dog will need ongoing physical therapy for up to a year to regain normal use of his leg. If both legs require surgery, wait to have the second surgery after full function has returned to the first leg.

COLLAPSED TRACHEA

The trachea, or windpipe, is normally supported by rings of cartilage to maintain its rounded shape. If this cartilage becomes weakened, the trachea loses its normal

Visit the vet before you treat any serious illness you suspect your pup might have.

Did You Know?

Heatstroke is a deadly condition that occurs when a puppy's body either absorbs too much heat from the environment or creates too much heat while exercising. Some puppies can overheat even in cool conditions, especially those pups with pushed-in faces (known as brachycephalic breeds), such as Pugs. Take frequent breaks when playing in a warm environment, and stop altogether if your puppy can't seem to stop panting. If your puppy has trouble walking or standing, begins to vomit, or her mouth and tongue become dark red or purple, soak towels in cool (not cold) water and place them over her. Run cool water in her armpit areas and over her tongue, if she is fully conscious. Don't allow your puppy to drink a large amount of water, which may cause vomiting. Call your veterinarian immediately for advice on further care.

Don't diagnose your dog by yourself. Always consult your vet if you're concerned about your Maltese's health.

shape making a dog's normal respiration difficult. The precise cause of this problem is unknown, but it is believed to have a genetic component. It is more prevalent in certain breeds, including the Maltese.

Symptoms include labored breathing, coughing, a characteristically honking-sounding shortness of breath, fatigue and exercise intolerance. Excitement, exercise, drinking or putting pressure on the trachea can trigger a bout of coughing. The cough may be intermittent or chronic, and it is often worse in the daytime and subsides at night. Symptoms rarely develop until middle age, and elderly and obese dogs are more prone to develop it. X-rays can confirm diagnosis, which will show a narrowing of the trachea.

Mildly affected dogs can lead normal lives, but avoid stress and vigorous exercise and closely monitor your dog's weight. Medical therapy consists of various combinations of bronchial dilators, cough suppressants, Prednisone to reduce inflammation and antibiotics to treat tracheal infections.

Vets occasionally recommend surgical treatment, but the outcome is not always successful, as the condition does pose an additional anesthesia risk.

REVERSE SNEEZING

Reverse sneezing is common in toy breeds and is often confused with tracheal collapse. It is characterized by rapid breathing, wheezing, snorting and honking with the neck extended. It can be triggered by overexcitement, eating or drinking too quickly, or pulling on the leash. The pharynx goes into spasms causing a gag reflex. It usually subsides on its own in a few minutes and does not require medical treatment. If your dog starts reverse sneezing, keep him calm until the spasm stops. Sometimes, it helps to rub the dog's throat or cover his nostrils for a few seconds, forcing him to breathe through his mouth.

LIVER SHUNT

A liver shunt (or extrahepatic portosystemic shunt) denotes a variety of congenital malformations causing abnormal blood flow through the liver. Normally, the liver filters toxins and metabolizes nutrients as the blood circulates from the digestive tract into the liver and to the *vena cava* (the large blood vessel that circulates blood back to the heart). Malformation of a portosystemic shunt (PSS) causes blood to be "shunted" past the liver directly back to the heart. Nutrients cannot be utilized, and toxins are returned to the blood stream, where they eventually build up to dangerous levels.

PSS can produce variable symptoms depending on the amount of blood being shunted past the liver. The problem usually becomes obvious in puppies, and most affected dogs are diagnosed before 1 year of age. However, some affected dogs remain asymptomatic until adulthood, and it has been detected in dogs as old as 8 years.

Affected puppies usually fail to thrive or grow, and they lack normal energy, balance and coordination. They have chronically poor appetites and suffer intermittent vomiting, diarrhea or bouts of pica (the desire to eat nonnutritive substances). The severity of the symptoms may fluctuate, but they usually become more pronounced immediately after the puppy eats a protein-rich meal. The protein causes toxins to build up in the bloodstream, triggering neurological and behavioral abnormalities such as circling, head pressing, drooling and seizing.

Because their livers cannot normally metabolize drugs, affected dogs are often drug intolerant. Medications normally prescribed to control seizures may be potentially dangerous. Dogs are also known to have sensitivity to sedatives.

They are also prone to urinary tract infections characterized by increased thirst and frequent urination, crystal formation in the urinary tract and bladder stones.

Liver shunt diagnosis is confirmed by a combination

Schedule regular vet checkups to make sure your Maltese is in top condition.

of blood tests and liver function tests, as well as monitoring bile acid levels before and after eating. If these tests point toward a liver shunt diagnosis, your vet will use portal radiography to confirm it. This test is highly invasive, but it clearly shows the pathway of blood vessels into the liver and is necessary to evaluate the dog's potential for surgical correction. Depending on the severity of the defect, treatment may be surgical or medical. In surgery, the vet ties off the shunt to direct more blood flow into the liver. A low-protein diet may also help to minimize digestive toxins in your dog's bloodstream.

BLADDER STONES

Urinary calculi can form in any portion of the urinary tract, but dogs most frequently develop them in the bladder, earning the name "bladder stones." There are various types, but all are formed from minerals found in the urine. Beginning as tiny crystals, they can eventually reach 3 to 4 inches in diameter.

Several factors can cause a dog to form stones, including genetic predisposition, excessive amounts of protein in his diet, high pH levels in his urine and bacterial infections in his bladder.

Symptoms can include bloody urine, difficulty urinating or voiding very small quantities of urine. Sometimes affected dogs don't show any symptoms. You may not detect a problem until you take your dog in for a routine health exam. But once detected, the stones must be removed. Treatment depends on the stones' size, number and location. A stone causing complete urinary obstruction is painful and life-threatening. Emergency surgery is the only option.

Stones in the bladder can be removed surgically or medically. Medical treatment involves a combination of antibiotic therapy and dietary modification to dissolve the existing stones and prevent more from forming. Your vet will culture a urine sample to determine its pH level, the makeup of the crystals and the type of bacteria present. Once this is established, your vet can tailor the dog's diet and drug intake to correct the problem. Your vet may also prescribe urinary acidifiers or a diet low in protein; magnesium and phosphorous may be prescribed to dissolve existing stones and prevent crystal formation.

You can also add salt to your pup's diet for 60 to 150 days to encourage him to drink more water, which will help to flush his bladder and prevent crystal formation. After that time, you can control the problem daily using acidifiers and salted foods. You may need to continue preventive treatment indefinitely because recurrence is common in dogs once they have had bladder stones.

HYPOGLYCEMIA

Hypoglycemia, a rapid and potentially fatal drop in blood sugar, is most common in very small dogs and young puppies of lower than normal weight and minimal body size. Their livers cannot manufacture and store enough blood glucose to adequately supply their brains with energy. Normally, when the body's glucose supply is depleted, it utilizes energy reserves stored in fat. With no backup supply, the brain becomes starved for energy and begins losing normal function. The resulting symptoms include sudden weakness, incoordination and drowsiness. If it progresses, it may result in seizures, coma or death.

Hypoglycemic episodes require prompt treatment to restore the dog's normal blood glucose level. If your dog is conscious, give small sips of pediatric glucose solution or a mixture of Karo syrup and water. A high-calorie and vitamin dietary supplement paste made for pets or plain vanilla ice cream may also do the trick. If your dog is too weak to swallow or already losing consciousness, do not attempt to give him anything by mouth because he will choke or aspirate it into his lungs. Keep him warm

Did You Know?

A cost-conscious dog owner may find that pet health insurance is a good idea. It can be a good way to limit your costs on veterinarian bills, particularly if the insured dog is a puppy. If you're interested in purchasing health insurance for your new pup, now's the time to sign it up; at least under some plans, your costs will be cheaper than if you wait till your puppy reaches adulthood.

Sudden weakness, incoordination and drowsiness could all be signs of canine hypoglycemia. When in doubt, have a vet check your Maltese's blood glucose level.

and transport him to the nearest emergency clinic for treatment.

If your Maltese is at a high risk of hypoglycemia, feed him frequent, small meals that are high in protein, fat and carbohydrates. Never allow your pup to miss a meal; make sure he is supplemented after any vigorous exercise. This is especially important for young puppies after lively play sessions.

Physical problems like fleas or intestinal parasites can also cause stress and trigger attacks. Avoid subjecting your dog to chilling, anxiety or overexcitement. Most dogs outgrow hypoglycemia as they grow and gain weight and as their liver functions catch up to their brains' energy demands.

PATENT DUCTUS ARTERIOSUS

Dogs are prone to developing a number of heart defects, and Maltese are no exception. Patent ductus arteriosus is the most common. It has been documented in many breeds, but Maltese are at an especially high risk. All puppies are born with a small blood vessel — the ductus arteriosus — linking the pulmonary artery and the aorta. Prior to birth, this vessel allows blood to circulate, bypassing the lungs.

After birth, the puppy's lungs become functional, and the blood circulation begins carrying oxygen from the lungs throughout the body. At that point, the ductus arteriosus typically closes off, but it sometimes doesn't close off completely in some dogs. The resulting defect may be minor — a small pocket off of the aorta. In more serious cases, the opening remains large enough to continuously shunt blood between the right and left ventricles of the heart. The severity of the symptoms will vary depending on the formation of the

A puppy's body weight is 60 percent water, so even a small loss of body fluid, such as that resulting from vomiting or diarrhea, can cause dehydration. If you suspect your puppy is dehydrated, offer her cool, clean water or an unflavored electrolyte solution such as the type marketed for human babies. If your puppy refuses to drink or seems otherwise depressed, vomits or has diarrhea, or has a high or low body temperature, take her to a veterinarian immediately.

defect. Eventually, it may lead to congestive heart failure.

The vet can usually detect a characteristic heart murmur during a routine exam long before other symptoms appear. Depending on the nature of the defect, a veterinarian may be able to treat the condition medically or surgically. Surgery is usually performed as early as possible before the occurance of changes that are commonly associated with heart disease.

MITRAL VALVE DISEASE

Weakness of the valves between the heart chambers permits blood to leak between the heart's chambers and compromises its pumping power. Mitral valve disease is common in all dogs 10 years or older, but some breeds (including the Maltese) develop it at a younger age due to genetic predisposition.

The first sign is a heart murmur detected during routine examination. This, in itself, isn't a major cause for concern and doesn't always progress to serious heart disease that will affect the dog's quality of life. Treatment will depend on whether the murmur is mild

(grade 1) or severe (grade 6). A grade 1 or 2 may merit close observation. If it progresses to grade 3 or 4, the murmur will become louder, and your dog will develop symptoms such as intolerance for exercise and coughing due to fluid accumulation in the lungs. At this stage, your vet might prescribe diuretics to control fluid buildup and vasodilators to improve his heart's pumping action.

SENIOR CARE

Thanks to preventative care and advances in veterinary medicine, our pets are living longer, healthier lives. The Maltese is noted for his longevity, and you can happily expect to enjoy his companionship for up to 14 years. However, as he ages, your Maltese is apt to experience a range of physical and mental changes.

In his senior years, your Maltese may need changes in his grooming routine if his skin becomes drier and more sensitive. Less frequent bathing will prevent his skin and coat from drying out. He may also benefit from a moisturizing conditioner or fatty acid supplement to restore natural oils in his skin to good condition. Loss of muscle mass and bone density is also part of the aging process. This may not be obvious in a long-coated breed. Stiff joints and back trouble can indicate the onset of arthritic inflammation of the joints or spine. This can make an older dog reluctant to engage in normal exercise. He may become hesitant to go for a walk, climb stairs or jump off furniture. You may notice that he has trouble getting comfortable at night or suffers pain and stiffness when he first gets up in the morning.

A softer bed, orthopedic cushion or heating pad can make your senior dog feel more comfortable. If he has trouble maintaining his footing on slippery floors, move him to a carpeted area or set out throw rugs. Consult with your vet about possibly supplementing your dog's dietary changes or prescribing medication to alleviate joint or back pain.

Your dog's deteriorated sight or hearing can also affect his normal range of mobility. The most common visual change affecting older dogs is cataracts. Dogs are adept at compensating for vision loss, especially if it happens gradually. It may not become apparent until it is fairly advanced. He may have no trouble navigating around his normal surroundings but will become disoriented if anything is changed or if you take him to an unfamiliar place.

Likewise, the early signs of hearing loss may go undetected. He might fail to come when called or begin to disobey your cues. He may become difficult to rouse from a deep sleep or may be startled or fearful when touched or moved while asleep. Another common symptom of hearing loss is unexplainable chronic barking from a formerly quiet dog.

These physical problems can lead to several changes in behavior. Dogs that suffer from vision or hearing loss are at great risk of getting lost. They might wander away and quickly become disoriented in a normally familiar area. They also won't be aware of surrounding dangers, such as oncoming traffic. Also, physical disability or pain that impedes a senior dog's mobility can cause mental stress. If your Maltese is used to following you around the house, he may become agitated if he can no longer do that. The change in

mobility can also make it difficult for him to get away from stressful situations.

Housetraining lapses are another common problem in geriatric dogs. This can be due to a physical reason such as kidney disease. You may need to walk him more often than you used to. Joint pain, vision loss or increased sensitivity to inclement weather can make an elderly dog reluctant to go out. You may need to accompany him when he goes out, if he typically accesses your yard through a pet door, or you might need to provide closer access to an indoor elimination spot.

Maltese are a long-lived breed, and you'll need to accommodate yours during her senior years.

EQUALS FUEL

Every vet, breeder, trainer and dog-food company executive has something to say on the subject of canned, dry, natural, raw, organic and commercial dog foods. Sifting through all of this information to decide what is best to feed your Maltese can be challenging, to say the least.

It's easy to be impressed by claims of "natural," "healthy," "flavorful," "nutritious" or "veterinarian approved." In reality, many of these claims are meaningless, which makes differentiating the truth from the gimmicks a difficult task. Dog food manufacturers are required to include specific information on their labels. So, although it is best to ignore certain aspects of labeling, carefully scrutinize others.

First, you should make sure the ingredients (the nutrient profile) bear the Association of American Feed Control Officials approval. Only AAFCO-approved formulas can be

Averaging just 4 to 7 pounds, Maltese have small stomachs, which can't hold much food. Factor in their notoriously picky appetites, and finding a food that's packed full of nutrients becomes difficult. It probably means you'll have to spring for a higher-quality food. Why? Less-expensive foods usually consist of lower-quality ingredients that aren't as palatable, digestible or nutritious.

it's a **Fact**

labeled as "complete and balanced," meaning they meet the nutritional standards for dogs at various stages of life. Manufactures can prove their foods meet AAFCO standards in a variety of ways. The preferred testing method is by conducting strictly controlled feeding trials. The testing procedure also should be stated on the label. Prior to 1985, Beagles were used exclusively for these studies, but many manufacturers now have formulas tailored for large and small dogs.

This doesn't mean, however, that every AAFCO-approved food is fine for your Maltese. Foods with seemingly comparable nutritional levels can differ substantially. The "guaranteed analysis" on the label states the minimum amount of fat and protein and the maximum amount of crude fiber, ash and moisture.

The nutritional content can come from many sources of varying quality. A high-protein food could be created from a plant or an animal protein, which makes a big difference. All commercial dog foods contain meat and grains. Dogs are omnivorous and require some carbohydrates, but feeding meat-based formulas is preferable to giving your dog those containing high proportions of cereal. Discerning the relative amounts of each can be tricky.

DECIPHERING THE CONTENT

AAFCO-approved formulas must list ingredients in descending order based on their relative percentages by weight. This gives you some idea of the food's make up, but it's still confusing because ingredients with high water content (like meat) have greater relative weight than dry ingredients. Look for foods with a ratio of more meat-based ingredients.

Grain-based ingredients made from whole grains are preferable to grain byproducts. The most common are rice, wheat, corn, oatmeal, soy and barley. Many breeders recommend avoiding soy and wheat in favor of rice or potato for Maltese with food allergies. Some Maltese are also known to be intolerant of poultry products. Therefore, beef and lamb are preferred over chicken and turkey.

Meat, meat byproducts, meat meal and meat-flavored foods sound similar to each other, but each is a drastically different product. Meat meal and meat byproducts are derived from less-attractive animal protein sources like skin, organs, fatty tissue, feet and heads. Byproducts are not heat processed. They are typically found in canned food. Meat meal, which is derived from the same sources, is heat processed to remove fat and water during kibble manufacturing. To produce a uniform mixture, meat ingredients must be dehydrated and ground to a fine meal before mixing them with the cereal ingredients.

The most popular types of food among pet owners are canned and dry varieties. Most dog owners are less interested in semimoist foods because they contain high amounts of starch, sugar, artificial dyes, preservatives and synthetic flavorings. Semimoist foods aren't recommended for Maltese. Avoid any foods that contain artificial dyes, in particular, because they can contribute to the dog's allergies, tear staining and coat discoloration.

Believe it or not, during your Maltese's lifetime, you'll buy a few hundred pounds of dog food! Go to **DogChannel.com/Club-Maltese** and download a chart that outlines the cost of dog food.

CANNED FOODS

The advantages of canned food are variety, taste appeal and long shelf life. Unlike dry foods, they usually don't contain artificial preservatives. The ingredients are sealed and cooked at a high temperature that sterilizes the mixture in the can, preserving it until it's opened. Canned foods are relatively more expensive than dry foods because they contain approximately 75 percent water, compared to dry foods that have about 10 percent. That also means a small dog must consume relatively more food to meet his nutritional requirements. Most canned foods contain about 8 to 15 percent protein and 2 to 15 percent fat.

Canned food's taste appeal is a definite advantage, but it won't help prevent tartar buildup like eating dry foods will. One way to solve this dilemma is to use small amounts of canned food to flavor dry kibble. Add just enough wet food to flavor the dry food without changing its texture.

DRY FOODS

Although dry foods are not available in as many varieties as canned foods, there are some specially formulated for toy breeds. These are made of smaller-sized kibble with concentrated amounts of nutrients per serving to accommodate toy breeds' smaller stomach capacities in relation to their body weight.

A drawback of some dry foods is their higher amounts of carbohydrates and inferior sources of protein. The starch content can be 40 to 60 percent compared to canned foods, which are 1 to 2 percent starch. Dry foods also contain preservatives. Because fat can't be mixed into the formula during cooking, it is added afterward as a coating. Preservatives must also be added to prevent the dry food from becoming rancid. Kibble stays fresh for about three months once you open it.

Commonly used synthetic preservatives such as butylated hydroxyanisole, butylated hydroxytoluene and ethoxyquin are FDA-approved, but they remain controversial because of potential health risks. Some are suspected to cause autoimmune disorders, reproductive disorders and even cancer. Maltese have been known to have allergic reactions to dry foods, and many breeders recommend avoiding them. Some kibbles are naturally preserved with vitamins E or C, but they tend to have a shorter shelf life.

The crunchy texture of kibble can help control tartar. It produces a mechanical brushing effect on the tooth surface and helps reduce calcium levels in saliva, which is a major component of dental plaque, but that isn't the only reason why texture, size and shape of the kibble are important: Small dogs can choke on large kibble, and donut-shaped kibble has been known to get wedged onto small dogs' canine teeth.

LIFE-STAGE FOODS

Growth formula (for puppies) and maintenance formula (for adults) are the only life-stage varieties that are AAFCO-approved, although others are also on the market.

If you have multiple pets, be sure each has her own food and water bowl. Sharing can lead to problems.

Puppy diets: Growth formulas must provide levels of fat and protein to sustain normal growth. The AAFCO requires that they contain a minimum of 22 percent protein, but some are much higher (sometimes contain up to 28 percent protein and 18 percent fat). Maltese experience major growth by 4 to 5 months of age and reach adult size by 6 months. High levels of fat, protein, vitamins and minerals may not be necessary after that. Generally, a Maltese puppy should eat growth formula four times per day until 3 months of age, then eat it three times a day until 6 months old. After that, switch your pup to an adult food.

Some puppies temporarily lose their appetites during teething, between 4 to 6 months of age. During this time, you may want to offer your pup softer foods or supplement his diet with a daily tablespoon of cottage cheese or yogurt to ensure he gets adequate calcium.

Adult diets: AAFCO-approved adult-maintenance diets must contain at least 18 percent protein and 5 percent fat. This is ideal for a normally active Maltese.

NOTABLE & QUOTABLE

We never use plastic [food or water] bowls. Breeders have found that, if they feed out of stainless steel or ceramic bowls, Maltese' noses don't lose their black pigment.

— breeder Joanne Boyles of Cranberry Township, Pa.

Water is one of the most important and often overlooked aspects of a healthy diet. Your Maltese must have a supply of clean, fresh water at all times. Tap water is a controversial topic among Maltese breeders. If you normally don't drink your tap water, don't give it to your dog either. Local water with a high mineral content can exacerbate tear-staining problems, and Maltese can suffer digestive upsets from unfamiliar tap water. Use bottled water at first and gradually add more tap water over a period of 10 days.

The breed does not require higher levels of fat and protein found in formulas for performance or high stress. These can contain up to 30 percent protein, 20 percent fat and 1,750 calories per pound. The dog's liver and kidneys will work overtime metabolizing excessive protein, and the high fat content can cause digestive upsets and obesity. A normally active adult Maltese should eat twice a day.

Senior diets: Your dog's nutritional needs may change after age 7. An older, sedentary Maltese may need fewer calories, smaller kibble, softer-textured food or a formula containing lower levels of sodium and fat. But consult your vet or breeder before feeding a senior diet. A senior Maltese may need fewer calories but still needs sufficient protein to maintain muscle mass. There is no nutritional profile established by the AAFCO for geriatric diets, and they can range from 18 to 27 percent protein and 9 to 12 percent fat. Some may contain protein and fat levels higher than maintenance formulas, neither of which is good for an elderly dog suffering from kidney problems or obesity.

Senior dogs can be reluctant to accept dietary changes, so don't switch unless it is warranted. If your older Maltese begins gaining or losing weight, check with your vet to rule out any underlying health problems. Reluctance to eat can result from tooth decay. Elderly dogs may need more time to eat their usual amounts. Splitting daily rations into three or more smaller meals may help.

SPECIAL DIETS

Low-calorie diets: Light-formula foods have become popular as America's pets get fatter. A tiny Maltese can put on weight very quickly. Obesity can contribute to heart and liver problems, pancreatitis, diabetes, arthritis, bladder cancer and skin disorders, and it can put a pet at a higher risk of dying while undergoing anesthesia.

The AAFCO hasn't established a nutritional profile for light foods, but the label must state exactly how much lower in fat or calories the food is compared to the regular formula. Most contain 25 percent protein

Feeding your Maltese is part of your daily routine. Take a break, have some fun online and play "Feed the Maltese," an exclusive game found only on **DogChannel.com/Club-Maltese** — just click on "Games."

JOIN OUR ONLINE Club Maltese™

Dogs evolved by hunting and eating and eating other animals, not by grazing in wild cornfields. Animal proteins (including fish, egg, cheese, beef, lamb and poultry) remain the most appetizing and nutritious dietary ingredients. Meat costs a lot more than grains, and the cost is passed along to the consumer. The good news is that — even though you'll pay more per bag, can, frozen patty or batch of home-prepared food — the overall cost of feeding them remains reasonable because Maltese eat such small quantities.

and 5 percent fat. A pound of adult-formula dry food contains between 1,400 and 2,000 calories, and adult-formula canned foods contain 375 to 950 calories per pound. The maximum that the AAFCO allows for light foods is 1,409 calories per pound for kibble and 409 calories per pound for canned foods.

Keep in mind that a typical Maltese only needs 150 to 250 calories a day to maintain his optimum weight. Even a light food can contribute to obesity if you don't limit the portion size. These foods usually contain high levels of fiber to make them more filling. You can accomplish the same result by replacing part of your dog's normal portion with rice cakes or cooked carrots and green beans. However, doing this may cause nutritional deficiencies in tiny dogs. A low-fat senior-formula may be a better choice. It's best to consult your vet first before trying your own variations.

Of course, you can avoid canine obesity altogether by paying attention to your dog's diet and general condition. Many changing factors affect a dog's metabolism and caloric needs. Check your Maltese's weight and make small dietary revisions as needed. You should be able to feel your dog's ribs, and he should have some indication of a waistline. If there is a layer of fat around his chest, middle or back, it is time to cut back. On the other hand, if you can see his ribs and hipbones through his coat, he is underweight.

Natural Foods: We have become more conscious of the long-term risks and benefits associated with diet. By the same token, multiple dog food ingredients are suspected to cause health problems ranging from allergies to cancer. Understandably, we increasingly opt for pet foods labeled as "healthy," "natural" and "free of chemical additives." These can be ideal diets for your Maltese, if the food is really what it claims to be.

Some natural foods sell for more than double the price of premium brands. Read the food labels carefully before opening your wallet because some of the claims are actually meaningless.

Organic foods destined for human consumption must adhere to guidelines (such as no antibiotics, pesticides or synthetic ingredients) set by the National Organic Standards Board, a branch of the U.S. Department of Agriculture. However, these standards do not apply to pet foods because all dog food is regulated by the Food and Drug Administration, which has no official guidelines for organic food.

For that matter, dog food is not subjected to any FDA presale approval process because it is made from ingredients that are "generally recognized as safe" and from

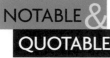

NOTABLE & QUOTABLE

I think dogs should eat dog food. If you never give them people food, they'll never know what they're missing.
I think they maintain better appetites because they're not holding out for something better to come along.

— breeder/owner Angela Stanberry of Ponchatoula, La.

additives that are approved by the FDA. No regulatory guidelines exist for foods labeled "natural," "human grade," "veterinarian approved" or "healthy." According to federal law, all commercial dog food must be pure, wholesome, free of harmful substances and truthfully labeled, but many statements on the packages can be meaningless or misleading despite complying with the law. Check the sources of the ingredients in the foods you buy for your dog to ensure the truth of these claims.

ADDITIVES

Most commercial foods contain one or more additive, such as vitamins and minerals, natural and chemical preservatives, or artificial ingredients to enhance color, flavor or texture. All of these additives are FDA approved, but it doesn't necessarily guarantee that they are harmless or healthy. Many food additives have been revealed as harmful long after receiving FDA approval.

Most Maltese breeders avoid foods containing chemical additives as much as possible because they may contribute to allergic reactions and tear staining. Any food containing color enhancers can cause generalized facial hair discoloration. As a rule, light-colored kibbles and treats are less likely to cause discoloration.

SUPPLEMENTS

Only give your Maltese supplements specifically recommended by your breeder or veterinarian. Despite the fact that they are sold on health food store shelves and over the counter in drugstores, there are potential risks associated with vitamins, minerals and herbal supplements.

If your dog's diet requires supplementation, never use products sold for human consumption. Properly calibrating the dose for a 5-pound dog can be tricky. Overdosing or improperly balanced supplementation can cause nutritional imbalances or vitamin toxicity. Some supplements can also adversely react with prescription medications.

Many supplements enter the retail distribution chain despite containing unapproved or impure ingredients or displaying false labeling. Use brands specifically for dogs that carry CL (Consumer Lab) or USP (United States Pharmacopoeia) endorsements.

GENERAL FEEDING TIPS

If you acquired your Maltese from a responsible breeder, you probably received detailed feeding information and a supply of food at the time of the purchase. If your dog is doing well on the diet, stick to it. These recommendations are based on extensive experience and research.

Consistency, rather than variety, is the basic rule of the successful Maltese diet. This applies to the type of food, portion size and routine. It is the best way to keep your dog at his ideal weight and to prevent bad eating habits.

Your dog's nutritional needs will change over the course of a lifetime, and it's up to you to ensure that his diet consistently contains the proper balance of protein, fat, carbohydrates, vitamins and minerals. If you need to switch foods, gradually replace larger portions of his regular diet with the new food over a period of seven to 10 days. Watch for changes in his appetite, health and condition during this time. Dietary changes can cause health or behavioral problems, although they might not become apparent for several weeks.

Portion control is equally important. The suggested amounts on dog food labels are only estimates. Two dogs of the same size may need different amounts to maintain their ideal weights. Likewise, you'll need to adjust the portions depending on your dog's age, metabolism, growth rate and activity level. Dogs usually consume their food within 20 minutes. Maltese, however, are known to eat slowly. This doesn't automatically mean your dog is overfed. By the same token, a dog that devours his food in 30 seconds isn't necessarily underfed. The recommended portions found on dog-food labels are broad guidelines. Evaluating your Maltese's present weight and condition is equally important when calculating his proper portion size.

A consistent feeding routine will foster good eating habits, a healthy appetite and good table manners. Feed your Maltese in the same place at the same time every day. A puppy may need three or four daily meals, and adults should eat twice per day. Remove the food after your dog has had sufficient time to eat it. Conditioning him to eat in a certain place discourages begging at the table. He will also be far less likely to pick at his food if he knows you're going to take it away after his mealtime. If he doesn't finish his food, don't offer him anything else until his next mealtime.

If you are concerned that your Maltese is not eating enough, take him to the vet for a checkup. If there is no underlying health problem, don't make matters worse! Don't be tempted to give your dog part of your dinner, cook any of *your* food especially for him or allow him to have treats *instead* of his normal food. Dogs are masters of mealtime manipulations. The end result will either be a chronically picky eater or a very fat Maltese.

TREATS AND SNACKS

Just like the rest of us, dogs enjoy occasional treats. This is fine, as long as you exercise a degree of self-control. Dogs don't become obese without help from their owners. Novice dog owners are especially guilty of giving too many treats. Treats should never comprise more than 10 percent of your dog's daily food intake.

Choose your dog's treats just as carefully as your choose his food. Many treats are comparable to junk food: difficult to resist but chock full of fat, sugar and artificial ingredients. Although they are not required to meet any AAFCO nutritional standards, all ingredients must appear on the labels. This also goes for chews like rawhides that dogs can potentially ingest.

Stick with brands made of natural ingredients or forego store-bought treats, and reward your Maltese instead using bits of cheese, pieces of fruit or plain, popped popcorn (with no butter or salt).

Did You Know? **Dry foods must contain a minimum of 40 percent carbohydrates (grains and starches) in order to bake into dry kibble.** Dry dog foods were invented about 50 years ago, primarily offering convenience (easy storage, low rate of spoilage, less messy to serve) and a lower-cost means of feeding dogs. Although they are not the most natural meals for dogs, when properly fortified with vitamins and minerals, dry diets provide a simple means of feeding a balanced diet — as long as you can find one that your dog will eat!

CHAPTER 9

MALTESE

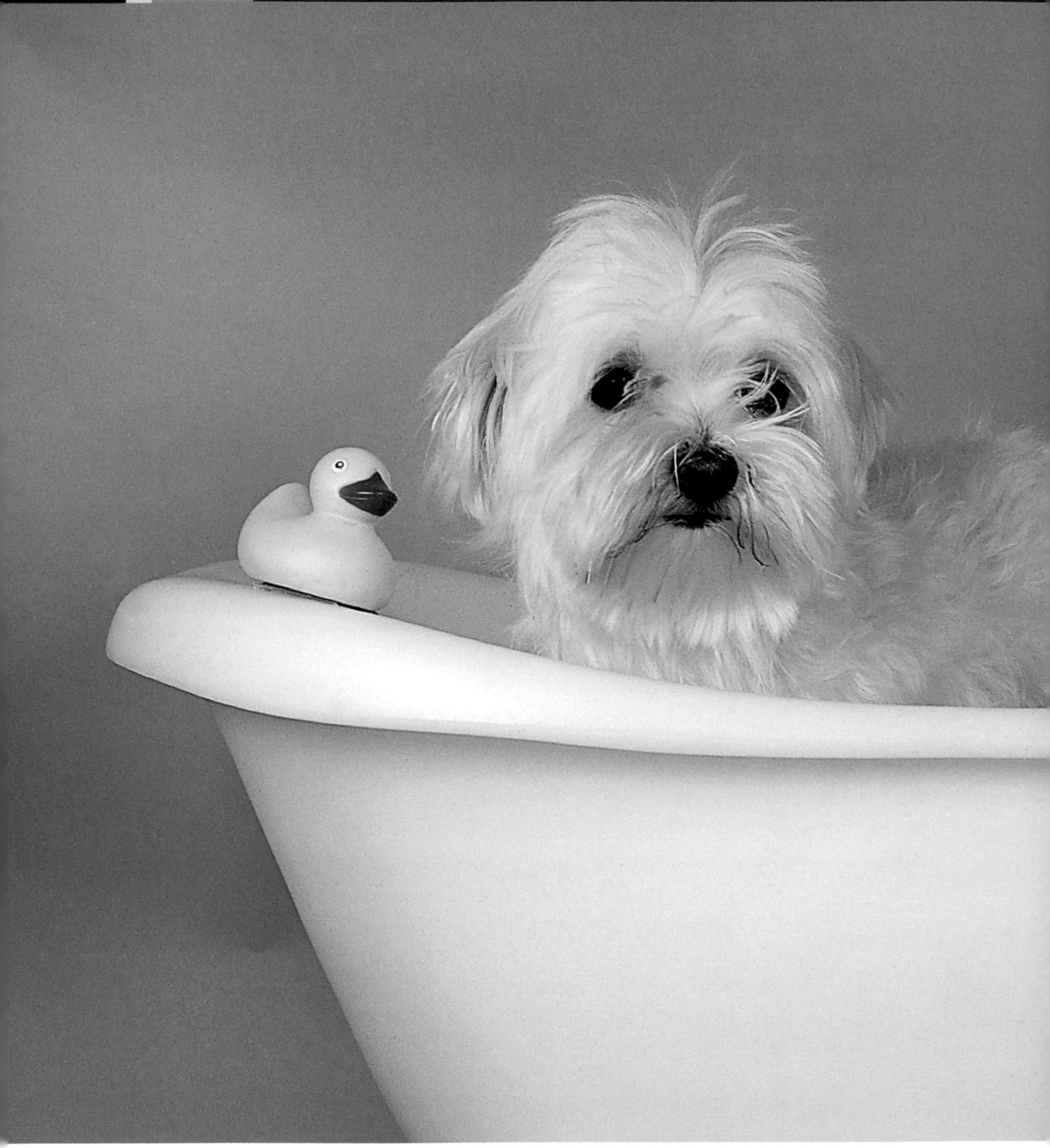

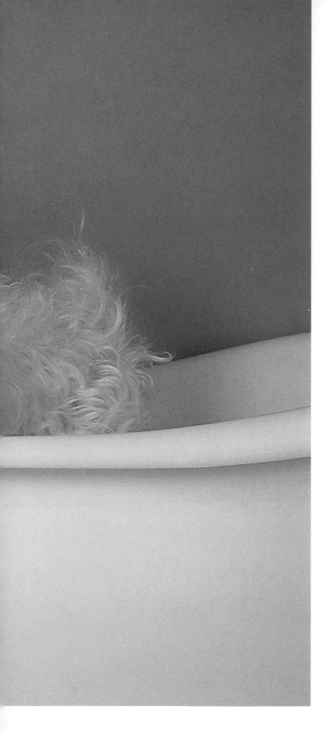

Maltese are one of those great breeds with little to no shedding, but that doesn't mean they don't still need to be regularly groomed. Since they have hair instead of fur and shed minimally, the hair will remain on your dog — waiting for the day you forget to take out the brush. Then the hairs will begin to wind together, creating a nasty tangle. Forget to brush your Maltese for two days, and more tangles will mysteriously appear. Go an entire week, and you will be in serious tangle trouble. Don't let grooming your Maltese become a daunting task. Keeping to a regular routine will stop problems before they start.

BRUSHING

You'll need a plan of attack when you brush your Maltese. Imagine a grid pattern on the dog and brush one grid at a time. Begin at the same place each time and part the hair into sections. Brush from the skin outward, but don't use the bristles directly on your dog's skin, which is usually sensitive. Hold each section of hair while you're brushing it to help brace the hair so the brush doesn't pull if it catches a tangle. If you do find a tangle, spray some detangler and separate the tangle with your fingers as much as possible. Then, work the brush through the snarl, following last with a comb. If the comb still sticks in the coat, go back with the brush again, taking care not to dig the brush bristles into your dog's skin. Repeat as necessary.

Run your comb through the entire coat one last time to verify all the tangles are gone. Once your dog is completely combed

out from his skin to the tip of his outermost hair, he's ready for a bath, if necessary.

BATHING

Before you start, gather together all of your bathing materials. Since your Maltese is small, you can stand and bathe him in your kitchen if you have a deep sink and a spray attachment.

Gently insert a cotton ball into each of your pup's ears to help keep water from entering his ear canals. Dilute the canine shampoo and conditioner to the consistency called for on the bottle. If you have a shower spray attachment, use it to completely wet your dog. When applying the shampoo, begin at the back of the head.

When washing his face, place a small amount of shampoo on your fingers and carefully wash the top of his head, ears and face. Take care not to get any soap in your dog's eyes. Use a washcloth to clean any debris from around his eyes.

Work the shampoo into your Maltese's coat very carefully, being sure not to rub the hair back and forth in a circular motion. This will cause the coat to tangle again. Use the spray hose or a plastic cup to thoroughly rinse the shampoo from his coat — especially if your home's tap water is soft. Soft water causes soap to lather more and makes it more difficult to rinse. Once all of the soap is washed away, apply a coat conditioner.

Maltese don't roll out of their crates looking marvelous. Routine grooming maintenance is a must.

The first thing I tell my clients [about typing a topknot] is to never use ponytail holders like the ones you use on children. Rubber bands cause hair breakage. Instead, purchase latex bands. — groomer Jay Scruggs in Germantown, Tenn.

Many Maltese owners take their dogs to professional groomers once a month for baths. While there, have your dog's anal area, stomach and footpads trimmed. The groomer will also clean out your dog's ears and trim her nails. Some even empty the anal glands during the bath. This tandem approach means you'll only have to concentrate on brushing and combing during the next month.

Squeeze the conditioner through your dog's hair, then rinse it out. Wrap him in a towel, but don't briskly rub him with the towel, as it will tangle his coat. Instead, continue to squeeze his hair with the towel in segments. Dry his legs, then the hair hanging from his body and so on until he is damp, not wet.

If you use a hair dryer, never use the hot setting. Dogs have thinner skin than humans, so test the air's temperature on the inside of your wrist first. Set your dog on the table or a comfortable place for drying. Point the hair dryer in one direction instead of moving it in a back-and-forth motion, which causes tangles. Blow the hair in a uniform direction taking care not to leave the hair dryer pointed at the same spot for too long, which can burn the skin. As your Maltese's hair dries, lift it with your brush while the air blows toward it. Once his coat is dry, brush and comb through the hair, checking for tangles.

NAIL CARE

Proper foot care is crucial to any dog's normal function. If your Maltese's feet are healthy, good care will ensure that they'll stay that way. If his feet are in less than perfect condition, conscientious care is even more important to prevent them from getting worse.

The main reason why many pet owners neglect their dogs' foot care is because their pets are uncooperative unless they have been trained to accept handling. You might be able to revise this attitude in a difficult adult Maltese by handling his feet every day, but you'll have to be patient and persistent. Turning your dog's nail trimming into a wrestling match will make things far worse. If there is no hope of revising his bad attitude, plan to pay frequent visits to your vet or groomer.

If your Maltese is still a puppy, handle his feet frequently so he becomes accustomed to it. Regularly check them for minor injuries, broken nails or debris wedged between his pads. Trim his nails every two weeks. Some dogs need it more often, some less. If you can hear your dog's nails clicking on the floor, they are getting too long. Long nails are sharp; they can scratch up your furniture, upholstery and skin. They can also break or tear if they get caught in your bedding.

NAIL-TRIMMING PROCEDURE

Items you will need for foot and nail care include scissor- or guillotine-type nail trimmers, clotting powder, a pair of small blunt-tipped scissors to trim hair between the footpads and a pair of scissors to trim the long hair on the feet. Even small dogs have thick nails. Never use any human-type nail clippers.

Incorporate nail trimming into your dog's weekly grooming routine. His nails will be softer and more pliable right after he's bathed. Either stand your dog on a table or hold him on your lap to trim his nails. If you are nervous about doing it the first time, have a helper get a firm, steady grip on your dog while you clip. It is very easy to drop a struggling dog or accidentally clip a nail too short. If your Maltese's nails are white, it will be easier for you to judge where to clip; you will be able to see where the dark vein ends inside the nail, called the "quick," ends. It's more difficult to see the quick on dark-colored nails, so trim just a tiny bit at a time until you gradually pare them back to a short length.

Dogs have no feelings in the tips of their nails. When done properly, the trimming procedure is painless. Regular trimming also decreases the risk that you might cut a nail too short. The quick will gradually recede in response to regular trimming. As the quick becomes shorter, you are less likely to accidentally nick it.

Don't forget to trim your dog's dewclaws, if he has them. They grow faster than the other nails and eventually grow in a circular pattern, piercing the toe pad. After clipping, nails are much sharper than usual until they wear down a bit. You can speed this up by filing them smooth with an emery board or nail file.

If you accidentally cut a nail too short, it will bleed, but this isn't a serious injury. Dip the nail in clotting powder or cornstarch, or apply ice and pressure until the bleeding stops. Don't rinse it with water, which will delay clotting.

Thick hair growing between your dog's foot pads will also compromise his normal foot function. Trim his footpads carefully with small blunt-tipped scissors. Trim the hairs evenly with the foot and never try to trim between the toes. Stand your Maltese on a table and round off uneven hair with a sharp pair of scissors. Stand him on a contrasting dark surface to more easily see what you are doing.

If clipping your dog's nails scares you, have the groomer show you how to do it properly.

EAR CARE

Several factors predispose Maltese to ear problems, but that doesn't mean they're inevitable. Diligent routine maintenance can prevent most problems, so check your dog's ears daily and clean them weekly.

The Maltese is a "drop-eared" breed, meaning the dog's ear leather hangs down over the opening of the ear canal. This trait is commonly found in breeds like poodles and spaniels that were meant to hunt in dense underbrush or retrieve from water.

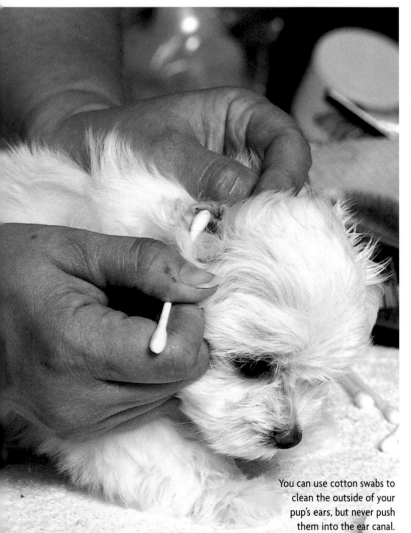

You can use cotton swabs to clean the outside of your pup's ears, but never push them into the ear canal.

The dropped ear protects the interior of the canal in those situations. Unfortunately, it also restricts the circulation of air inside the ear and creates a warm, moist environment that is ideal for infections.

The Maltese's frequent bathing needs also increase the possibility of moisture getting in their ear canals, which can lead to problems comparable to humans' "swimmers ear." Take steps to avoid getting water in your dog's ears while you bathe him, and always dry the ear coat and interior thoroughly afterward. Flush his ears with cleaning solution after every bath as a good preventative measure. Seasonal factors can also increase the likelihood of your dog having damp ears. Hot, humid weather or outings to lakes or pools merit the same extra care to ensure his ear canals stay dry.

Regularly remove excess hair growth in your dog's ear canals. It is a magnet for moisture, dirt and bacteria, making thorough cleaning even more difficult. Hold the ear flap open and sprinkle ear powder or baking soda onto any hair growing out of the ear canal. This will make it more brittle and easier to grasp. Use your fingers, a pair of tweezers or hemostat to grasp and remove it. Only pull a few hairs at a time, being careful not to pinch the skin. This hair will come out easily and painlessly. Don't try to remove the hair growing on the ear flap or around the ear, though.

If your dog's ears are clean, dry and odorless, they won't

NOTABLE & QUOTABLE

If you keep your Maltese in full coat, brush her hair daily using a good spray-on conditioner. If you find a lot of hair in the brush, it's probably broken hairs, signifying that her coat is drying out. You'll need to condition the coat to retain the moisture.
— groomer Jay Scruggs in Germantown, Tenn.

Be careful when brushing; Maltese are fair-skinned.
If you notice your brushing is making her skin bright pink in one spot, move on and go back to that spot the next day. You don't want to cause a sore or a skin irritation. Just as importantly, you do not want to cause your dog to associate grooming with pain. It should be a pleasant experience for both you and your pup.

need further attention. A small amount of yellowish ear wax is normal, but clean out his ears thoroughly if the wax is dark-colored or extensive. Use an ear-cleaning solution to flush the ears and loosen as much of the debris as possible. Hold the ear leather open and aim the nozzle of the bottle into the ear canal, but do not push it in the ear. Fill the ear with cleaning solution, close the ear flap and massage the liquid into the ear for a few seconds. Try not to let your dog shake his head; the solution could get into his eyes or yours. It's not harmful, but it will sting. Use cotton balls to wipe all resulting debris from the ear. Do it gently, but don't be hesitant about doing a thorough job.

Don't probe into your Maltese's ear. The canine ear canal is long and narrow, and bacteria or debris can become trapped inside, setting the stage for infection. If your dog's ears are very dirty, you may need to clean them every few days to get it under control.

Red, painful, irritated ears indicate a more serious problem that isn't going to respond to your diligent cleaning. Minor ear problems can quickly turn serious because they cause the dog so much dis-comfort. He will dig and scratch at his ears and shake his head. It is imperative to find out the cause before it results in a secondary infection or damage from scratching and head shaking, such as a hematoma when blood leaks from the vessel and pools in the ear tip.

Persistent ear problems may be a symptom of allergies or hypothyroidism. Ear mites might be responsible. Contrary to their name, they do not confine their activities to the ears. You'll need to treat the entire dog, his environment and other pets. Flea bites or ticks inside the ear can be the cause. They also require treating the dog and getting rid of the source. Burrs or seeds deep in the ear canal will cause ongoing trouble until they are removed, which can be difficult due to the shape of the canine ear canal.

Yeast and bacterial infections are the most common causes of canine ear troubles, and they can be very difficult to treat. The hallmark sign of a yeast infection is copious brownish matter and an unmistakable odor. As previously mentioned, the resulting irritation can lead to an eventual secondary bacterial infection.

Consult your vet for an accurate diagnosis if your dog is experiencing any ongoing ear problems.

TEAR STAINING

Tear stains (a reddish discoloration of the hair beneath the eyes, around the muzzle and sometimes on the feet) are a common problem for Maltese. They are basically a cosmetic problem, but your regular grooming should include treatments to keep your dog's eyes free of matter and the surrounding area dry. Moisture accumulating in the hair around they eye area can cause skin irritation or infection.

Be sure to brush your Maltese's long, fine hair after you let her play. It tangles easily and will be an unruly mess before you know it.

SMART TIP! **Use either the tip of a metal comb or a knitting needle to set a neat, straight part in the hair down your Maltese's back.** Begin at the base of her head, while looking down on your dog, and drag the comb along the spine to the base of her tail. Separate the part and brush the hair into place.

Wipe debris daily from the corners of your Maltese's eyes with a damp cotton ball or a premoistened eye-cleaning pad. Carefully comb the stained hair with a flea comb. Then, with a soft brush, apply cornstarch to the area to absorb the moisture. Comb through it so it doesn't cake up, and be sure to leave some powder on the hair. Some breeders recommend applying an ointment, such as petroleum jelly, to the hair around the eyes to repel water and keep the hair in place, but it's difficult to remove and can make matters worse if you don't keep your dog's face scrupulously clean. If his hair is long enough to fall into his eyes, trim it or keep it banded to prevent eye irritation.

To reverse tear staining, you must find the underlying cause. Tearing is normal, and all tears contain proteins that cause discoloration. When the dog produces tears faster than the tear ducts absorb them, the overflow causes wetness and staining.

There is also a hereditary component to the problem, which explains why some Maltese have more tear staining than others. It could be a combination of small tear ducts and very watery eyes. Facial features can also have an influence. Dogs with very large eyes and short muzzles tend to be more susceptible.

Eye irritation will intensify tear production. This can be due to wind, dust, pollen, tiny injuries or allergies. Rinsing your dog's eyes with mild boric acid eyewash two or three times a day may help, as long as you carefully dry the hair around his eyes after each treatment.

A dog's watery eyes may be due to a contact allergy to a grooming product or an allergy to a food, supplement or additive. Staining all over the face can be caused by drinking water with a high mineral content. Switching him to an additive-free food or bottled water may help. Ionizers and air filters can help lower the levels of dust and pollen in your home. Keeping your pup indoors when the pollen count is high may also help.

Secondary infections associated with tear staining can spread to other dogs in your home. Regularly wash and disinfect your dog's dishes, bedding and grooming equipment. Good ventilation, fresh air and sunshine are time-honored methods of sanitizing a dog's environment.

Dental problems or ear infections can also aggravate a dog's tearing. Puppies can develop tear staining during teething. Many breeders consider stress to be major cause of tear staining. If the problem has developed recently, consider a possible link to changes in your dog's lifestyle.

Treatment depends on the source of the problem but still includes a degree of experimentation. Breeders generally agree that surgery is *not* a recommended treatment to correct it. If all other causes have been ruled out, many vets prescribe a combination of eye drops and oral antibiotics. Low-grade ocular or systemic infections should respond to drug therapy. If a three-week dose of a broad-spectrum antibiotic fails, your veterinarian should culture your dog's

Clean around your Maltese's eyes daily to avoid tear staining — one of their most common grooming problems.

tear residue to identify the strain of bacteria. Randomly experimenting with various antibiotics or long-term use can lead to digestive problems and overgrowth of resistant bacteria.

Drug therapy will take about three weeks to stop the staining and will not remove discoloration, but new growth will be white. There is also a chance that the staining will resume once the antibiotics are stopped.

TINY TEETH

Pay attention to your dog's dental health, and you'll be rewarded with many extra years of life together. Small dogs are especially at risk for secondary complications due to periodontal disease if they develop tooth decay and gum infections. The bacteria in the gums can spread throughout the dog's body and shorten his lifespan.

Train your Maltese to accept a toothbrush with doggie toothpaste and a daily toothbrushing. Begin by massaging his gums and teeth with a piece of gauze wrapped around your finger. Gently rub the gauze against his gumline. Once your Maltese stops struggling against the gauze, switch to a toothbrush. Most dogs love the taste of doggie toothpaste and will accommodate the brushing process. When tartar builds up, consult your veterinarian about possibly scheduling a dental cleaning.

Setting the Maltese Topknot

Single Ponytail: Comb the hair from the midpoint of the skull forward. Part the hair from above the corner of her eye and pull it up to the middle. Hold the hair in one hand and do the same for the other side. Comb all the hair on top of the head into a ponytail and wrap a latex band around it. Carve an inverted "V" in the hair right behind the ponytail (with the point of the "V" facing the tail), pull it up and make a second ponytail. Hold this ponytail in your hand, then take the first section and pull it back. Secure both ponytails together with another band.

Double nubs: Gather the hair from mid-skull and comb it forward. Part the hair exactly down the middle, from the outside corner of the eye, and comb this hair together and secure it with a latex band. Do the same for the other side, then bend the ponytail in half, with the excess hair pointing toward the back, and secure it with another band. Repeat for the other side. You can attach a little bow over each nub if you want.

If the bands are too tight, loosen them by working the comb under the band and lifting slightly. Make sure that your dog can blink and that no skin is pulled up into the ponytail.

Don't get discouraged. Setting either of the topknot styles takes time, and it won't be perfect the first time you try. With practice, though, styling your dog's topknot will be a breeze.

OF TRAINING

Training may not have been a paramount concern when you chose this breed. Most owners acquire Maltese because they make wonderful companions, but that doesn't mean Maltese don't have the mental and physical capabilities for high-level training. Nor does their tiny size imply that training is unnecessary. Even if you don't have high show or sporting aspirations for your puppy, training will make him a far better companion.

Small dogs often have a reputation for being difficult to train. In reality, they can be trained just as easily as large dogs. The difference is that owners of larger breeds tend to approach the task more seriously. Large-breed puppies receive training more consistently beginning at a younger age. This may be based in practicality, but it's equally advisable for toy-breed puppies.

Every dog comes equipped with plenty of learning potential. Puppies begin teaching themselves about their environment as

Did You Know?

If your Maltese becomes anxious about something you're teaching her, you need to reduce the pressure. You may be working a little too fast. Break the exercise down into smaller pieces and be upbeat, then work through the problem. When you proceed at a pace your Maltese is comfortable with, you'll have a happy, willing student.

soon as they are able to climb out of the whelping box. They explore and experiment, and their mothers keep a close eye on them to make sure they don't get into trouble. By the time they are 5 or 6 weeks old, their breeders begin taking on the role of pack leader.

At this age, puppies are very responsive but not so good at remembering. Breeders usually spend a great deal of time teaching the pups basic housetraining and human social interaction. While providing crucial early socialization, it also introduces puppies to the concepts of training. Puppies learn some of these through interactions with other dogs, such as moderating their behavior to avoid conflicts, signaling their intentions before approaching another dog and gauging another dog's emotional state before approaching.

These social skills will also help in establishing the dogs' relationships with humans, which includes learning to conform to household rules. During these same weeks, the puppies' mother continues teaching them about canine social boundaries, doing things like reprimanding them when they bite or play too rough. In this way, a puppy is introduced to rules that will direct his canine/human interactions for the rest of his life.

By the time a Maltese puppy is 12 weeks old, he is equipped with some training and social skills, but he still needs a lot of practice to learn how to behave as an adult. At that point, it becomes an owner's responsibility to take on the role of pack leader, which includes teaching appropriate behavior. Don't expect your puppy to understand the rules and tools of successfully living with humans unless you take the time to teach him. Otherwise, he will develop his own ways to cope with everyday life. Many of which probably won't be to your liking, such as peeing on the rug, constantly barking at the neighbors or snapping at the groomer. Even if you aren't bothered by this misbehavior, it's unlikely that you are the only person that will have regular contact with your misbehaving Maltese. Other people are not going to appreciate it.

RENDEZVOUS WITH REALITY

Eventually, most owners get tired of their puppies' misbehavior. They might start berating their dogs out of frustration. The dogs in this situation, having never learned that their behavior is unacceptable, will be utterly confused and frightened. Keep in mind that the Maltese is a sensitive breed. Impulsive, emotional reactions in response to misbehavior will likely worsen existing problems, and that might not be the only complicating issue. What began as random misbehavior eventually evolves into an ingrained pattern of unwanted habits. Revising those patterns will require far more work than would have been needed to train the dog properly from the start.

As you can see, training is essential to raising a puppy. Be prepared to start training as soon as you bring your Maltese home. More importantly, be patient and don't expect instant results. The Maltese is also a

The best way to get your Maltese well socialized is to introduce her to different kinds of people and situations. Have her meet a man with a beard, take her to a dog-friendly restaurant, take her for a ride in the car. Go online to download a socialization checklist at **DogChannel.com/Club-Maltese**

very perceptive breed, but a puppy cannot be expected to learn and remember things after only one or two attempts. Don't make the mistake of thinking your puppy is reliably trained after a few successes. Training requires repetition and reinforcement, often until a puppy is a year old.

Some owners shy away from training, fearing it will undermine a puppy's trust and affection. This attitude is misguided and irresponsible. Regardless of whether you want a Rottweiler or a Maltese, don't get a puppy if you aren't willing to provide structure and leadership. Dogs are pack animals, and their mental stability depends on understanding the rules and boundaries of their packs. To a dog, having no pack rules means having no pack security. Your Maltese will be far more confident, secure and attached to you if you provide him with the consistency, structure and training that he expects from his pack leader.

COMMUNICATION

Setting and maintaining a rule structure doesn't imply that training alone will produce the perfect puppy. Training will be futile unless you first develop a strong bond and positive communication with your puppy. Owners sometimes fail to recognize the importance of these initial steps in the process. Bonding with your new Maltese will probably come quickly and effortlessly. He is pretty irresistible and definitely wants to please you. However, in order to please you, he needs to understand what you expect from him, and that requires straightforward communication.

Dogs don't come prepackaged with instructions. Following the advice in a canine training book won't accomplish anything unless your dog is paying attention while you train him. You must figure out the best way to gain and hold his attention. His ability to concentrate and remember will follow.

Your puppy must be calm, focused and attentive in order to learn. Canine training techniques are not one-size-fits-all. The approach you employ to achieve success depends on your dog's temperament. You must understand his personality and tailor your training methods accordingly. Learn to recognize and anticipate his typical reactions and communication signals. Growls, whines and barks can mean a lot of things when paired with a whole range of body and facial gestures.

Canine survival instincts have made dogs naturally attuned to interpreting our body language and vocal cues, so use the same sequence of words and gestures for specific cues. Speak in a soft, high-pitched tone for praise; a lower, quick tone for reprimands and a neutral tone when giving cues. Then, observe your dog's reaction to ensure he's paying attention to what you say. Some dogs are easily distracted by events in the environment, others try to turn every encounter into a game and a few become nervous and anxious — all these things will make it very difficult for a dog to pay attention and comprehend your meaning.

Training works best when incorporated into daily life. Whenever your Maltese asks for something, cue her to do an action she's learning, then reward by granting her request. Food isn't the only reward; anything your Maltese enjoys can be used as a reward.

it's a Fact

With the proper training, your Maltese will be as well behaved as she is adorable. One certification that all dogs should receive is the American Kennel Club Canine Good Citizen, which rewards dogs that have good manners. Go to **DogChannel.com/Club-Maltese** and click on "Downloads" to get the 10 steps required for your dog to be a CGC.

At this point, the prospect of dog training probably sounds very intense. Here's the good news: Playing with your puppy is an excellent way to forge trust and communication. It fosters a positive attitude about interaction with people. More importantly, it teaches you both the basics of interspecies communication. Take advantage of it. When done right, a rousing daily play session can serve as a major training tool. Just keep in mind that part of play includes setting boundaries by telling your puppy that behaviors like growling and nipping are unacceptable, even during play. This is exactly the type of feedback he expects from other dogs during play. If he accidentally nips or bites you while you're playing — whether or not he actually hurts you — stop the game, reprimand him and ignore him until he gets the message.

POSITIVE REINFORCEMENT

Setting boundaries and reprimanding unwanted behavior are important aspects of training, but they are not nearly as important as rewarding good behavior. Positive reinforcement is often considered a technique reserved for formal training. This is a mistake. Don't forget to praise your puppy whenever you catch him doing something right! This includes things like coming when called, cooperating for a grooming session or sitting quietly and playing with a toy while you are on the phone. All these behaviors deserve verbal praise and petting.

Positive reinforcement also includes using food rewards to encourage desirable behavior. Some owners worry that giving food rewards amounts to nothing more than bribery, deciding that a good dog should want to please his owner without expecting a payoff. Your Maltese certainly wants to please, but habit formation and memory are

major components of training. And canine memory skills tend to be somewhat selective. There is a biological reason for why dogs learn some things effortlessly, like where you keep the treats, while other lessons require endless repetition and practice. If a behavior is linked to a survival need, the dog will remember it much more quickly Rewarding with food creates a strong mental association because dogs are hard-wired to remember actions associated with their survival needs.

Food rewards are, therefore, very useful when you need to reinforce complicated training procedures like housetraining. Treats for a job well done encourage a dog to form a positive association much faster than it would otherwise happen. You may need to use a lot of treats when first teaching your pup something new and relatively complex. Once he gets the idea, an occasional treat will reinforce it. The trick is to avoid handing out treats predictably or indiscriminately. If he never knows for sure when the next reward's coming, he'll be far more focused.

DISCIPLINE

Training encompasses more than rewarding your puppy when you find him indulging in good behavior. You'll also need to address his unwanted behaviors in no uncertain terms. Maltese are sensitive and eager to please. Knowing that you are displeased with his behavior is usually enough to get the message across. Like all dogs, your Maltese is intent on retaining his favored position in your pack. Dogs are adept at forming associations between human responses and their actions. The trick to effective discipline is to make sure he forms the right connection. For instance, reprimanding your puppy after the deed is done will be pointless. He will know that you are very upset but won't connect your reaction to the table leg he chewed or the rug he peed on five hours ago. Scolding will only be effective if you catch him in the midst of the criminal act. If you do catch your puppy misbehaving, look him in the eye and sternly tell him "no, bad dog." Then ignore him for a while to make sure he gets the point.

Teaching your puppy to respect your authority when you tell him "no" is the best crime deterrent. It is far more preferable to constantly scolding him when he gets into mischief. Learning how to tell your puppy "no" in an effective way will actually limit the number of times you will ever need to do it. If he doesn't take you seriously, however, then he'll consider you saying "no" as an ongoing way for him to test the boundaries of your authority. You will end up resorting to it more often, and he will simply tune you out. Eventually, it will seem more like nagging than actual training.

Reprimand your pup correctly the first time. Make sure he pays attention, understands your message and complies. You must respond to unwanted behavior authoritatively and immediately. The purpose is not to frighten or hurt your dog. Your goal is to make him realize that his behavior has put him out of favor with his pack leader, which is a prospect that any dog will dread.

Don't be loud or rough, but make sure your voice has a serious, assured tone. A weak reprimand is worse than none at all. On the other hand, don't overdo it. Maltese don't need harsh discipline. Do it right, and do it once. Then ignore him for a little while afterward. When you think your pup's had sufficient time to get the point, reassure him that all is forgiven. This step is equally critical to the process. Most importantly, don't use your dog's name when reprimanding him. It's an easy habit to get into and will send mixed messages. Use his name only in positive contexts, such as when you're praising him or teaching him a new cue.

Training is essentially a psychological process. Using psychology to convince your dog that he wants to comply is far more effective and lasting. The keys to accomplishing this goal are short, upbeat train-

Food treats, given in moderation, can keep your Maltese focused on training.

ing sessions and lots of practice. Five-minute practice sessions for two or three times a day will work wonders. Puppies especially may become bored with long, intensive lessons. They don't possess the maturity or mental skills to remain focused for long periods of time. At best, your puppy will stop paying attention, or he may become stressed and intimidated. He might begin exhibiting typical signs of anxiety like panting, shaking and refusing to make eye contact, or he might start to engage in displacement behaviors like nonstop ear scratching or floor sniffing.

A good way to keep your Maltese interested in training is by breaking up the routine or introducing new challenges like the dog sports of agility or rally. More importantly, it will do wonders for your communication and teamwork.

TRAINING CLASSES

For consistency's sake, start incorporating home training into your puppy's daily routine from the first day you get him. Group training classes can be a great complement to your training at home. Once your Maltese has completed his puppy vaccinations, you can enroll him in a class. Try to find one that specializes in puppies or small breeds. Large, mixed classes are fine for most dogs, but they're not the ideal choice for a small, sensitive breed like your Maltese.

A chaotic, rowdy atmosphere can potentially do more harm than good. Your best bet is to ask other Maltese owners for personal recommendations for a good group training class. If that's not possible, ask permission to observe a class before signing up. This will ensure that the instructor's methods meet your approval and that the environment is safe and inviting for a small dog.

Your Maltese should look forward to attending his classes. If he doesn't, something is wrong. Perhaps the instructor is using the wrong approach or the classroom atmosphere is intimidating for your small dog. Keep looking until you find a class that fits his needs.

Group training classes offer puppies a much wider range of socialization opportunities with other people and dogs. Regular interaction with other dogs is essential to a well-rounded canine education, but accomplishing this can be tricky for a tiny Maltese puppy. Unlike random public encounters with other dogs, which can turn dangerous if not properly supervised, a training class provides a structured setting. Every canine interaction will be monitored by a professional trainer, who can intervene if necessary. Having that knowledgeable, experienced trainer present is the biggest benefit of joining a group class. You'll have expert advice readily available for any training problems that might arise. An experienced trainer will also be able to spot budding behavior problems before they present a serious training issue.

Puppy kindergarten classes are an ideal choice for introductory Maltese puppy training. They tend to be less formal and place greater emphasis on socialization.

The program is designed to accommodate a puppy's inexperience and short attention span. Another good option is a class limited to small dogs. Try to find one of those kinds of classes before enrolling your puppy in a class with a mixed group of large dogs and owners of varying skill levels.

The class should be a fun experience for both of you, but that isn't the main agenda. It's meant to enhance your training skills and improve your dog's ability to pay attention despite distractions. You will receive an introduction to basic cues: sit, stay, heel, come and down. The instructor should also provide individual attention for each handler/dog team. These weekly demonstrations of training techniques won't accomplish much unless you follow them up with practice at home. Your ultimate success will depend on the amount of time and work you put into it.

LEASH TRAINING

Leash training a tiny Maltese puppy may seem unnecessary, but failing to do so is a mistake. Dogs of all breeds respond to this training much more readily at a young age; they adapt much easier to the sensation of wearing a collar. A little puppy is also more likely to follow his pack leader willingly without questioning why. As he gets older, the process will take longer.

Leash training actually involves teaching several training skills. Learning to accept the lead, walk at your side and ignore distractions is a lot for a puppy to take in. Break up the lessons and teach only one at a time.

Begin introducing your puppy to a lightweight buckle collar or harness and lead by 12 weeks of age. That is quite enough for his first lessons. After a few days, start attaching the lead. Let him drag it around

Toys, treats or anything else your pup loves can be great training tools.

the floor, or hold it and let him walk wherever he wants to. Do not apply pressure to the lead or try forcing him to follow you. Be sure to lay on the praise and encouragement, when appropriate.

Depending on your puppy's personality, adapting to the collar may take anywhere from a day or two to several weeks. Some puppies will be ready to go as soon as you put the lead on them; others may be very sensitive to it. Once your dog is comfortable with the equipment, start encouraging him to take a few steps. Coax him with toys, treats and a lot of praise until he feels confident enough to walk with you. At that point, you are well on your way. Walk a little farther each day, and don't be surprised if he becomes ecstatic as soon as he associates when it's time for a walk.

Keep the lessons short, and don't begin walking your dog in busy, crowded areas until he feels completely confident with this part of the training. If something frightens him during a walk, he may panic and try to

Teaching a dog to heel makes going for walks much more enjoyable.

pull away. There's a possibility that he could slip out of his lead and run away. A scare can also cause your pup to form a phobic reaction to the restraint of the lead. Use plenty of positive reinforcement, and give him as much time as he needs to do this.

Once your puppy is walking reliably, begin teaching him to heel. Your goal is to teach him to walk calmly at your side, maintaining your pace on a loose lead. A dog that is constantly lunging, jumping and weaving back and forth is annoying and can be dangerous to himself and his owner.

The simplest solution is to keep your dog from starting this habit in the first place. As soon as your puppy begins pulling ahead of you, just stop. At first, he will probably be surprised and confused. But he will soon learn that you consistently walk only when he maintains a normal pace on a loose lead. If you start allowing him to drag you down the street, it will only get worse.

You can also reinforce a proper speed by keeping treats in your hand or pocket and rewarding him for maintaining the desired pace. He will soon learn that keeping pace with you is worthwhile. Don't forget to praise him when he walks politely on lead at the proper speed.

Positive reinforcement is far more preferable to jerking on the lead as a corrective measure. Many dogs instinctively respond to the negative reinforcement by pulling even harder, and a delicate breed such as the Maltese could easily be injured in the

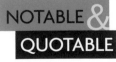

NOTABLE & QUOTABLE

I've learned that, if I push too hard, they become discouraged and shut down on me. Compared to a lot of breeds, I think the Maltese's personality is somewhat softer because they want to please you so much. I try to make it more fun and break down what we're working on into smaller pieces they can succeed with.

— *Lynn Berry of Winston-Salem, N.C., agility competitor*

process. Using psychology is always preferable to confrontation.

CUEING BEHAVIORS

Come: Teaching your puppy to come when he's called is another example of reinforcing a natural inclination. Puppies generally learn their names without the benefit of formal training or reinforcement. They also come running to greet you without needing lessons. Your Maltese puppy has a natural instinct to do these things, but it doesn't mean he actually understands the concept of coming when he's called.

Begin teaching your pup to come on cue as soon as he learns his name. One of the easiest ways to accomplish this is by giving the cue when he's already heading toward you. Get down to his level, say "come" and coax him toward you with a combination of treats, toys and verbal encouragements. Vary the location and have other family members practice with him, too. Your goal is to create a reliable response in a variety of situations. It takes a lot of practice before a puppy forms completely reliable responses to your cues. Reinforcement consists of randomly calling and rewarding him for no particular reason. Don't jump to premature conclusions after a few successful experiences.

Another common mistake is to follow up this cue with something the dog doesn't like. Calling him to come in for dinner is one thing. Calling him for a bath is another matter. Needless to say, never use this cue or his name in conjunction with a scolding. Any type of negative reinforcement is totally counterproductive when teaching the come cue.

If your Maltese refuses to come or, worse yet, he starts moving in another direction, don't lose your temper or chase him. Use psychology instead. Ignore him or walk away. Sooner or later, he'll follow you. As soon as he does, repeat the cue and follow up with praise and a reward. Teaching your Maltese to come when he's called can save his life if he ever gets loose or runs away.

Sit: Start teaching your puppy to sit when he is about 10 to 12 weeks old. Simply hold a treat in your palm at his eye level and slowly raise it over his head; you're luring him into the desired position. As his head follows your hand up and back, his hind end will go down. You can help, if necessary, by gently using your other hand to guide him into a sitting position. As soon as you see him start to sit, tell him "sit," then give him the treat and plenty of praise. Once he begins to associate your hand gesture with an imminent reward, you can utilize that signal.

Down: The same method can be utilized to teach him the down cue. Hold a treat in your palm in front of his nose. Slowly lower it to the floor and simultaneously pull it away from him. Usually, he will scrunch down to try to get the treat. You can encourage this by moving the treat away and keeping it mostly hidden in your palm. Teaching "down"

Regular play and exercise sessions will help build your dog's confidence and bond her to you.

may take more time because there are so many floor-level distractions for a tiny Maltese. This is especially true for a young puppy with a short attention span.

Stay: Once your puppy responds fairly reliably to your sit and down cues, you can start teaching him to stay. Make sure he is tired and reasonably calm before introducing this lesson, and keep him on lead when you first teach the cue. Tell him to sit and follow with the cue word "stay." It may help to combine the cue with a hand signal.

Back away from your dog one or two feet while still holding the lead in your hand. Be ready to reposition him when he moves. At first, be satisfied if your pup stays in place for a few seconds. At that point, give him a release cue, such as "ok," and reward him. As he gets the hang of it, use your judgment in extending the length of time and your distance from him.

The trick is to keep this a very positive experience for your puppy. Don't try to intimidate him into staying still. Make it fun and upbeat. As soon as he learns that doing nothing will earn a reward, he will become cooperative. But don't push your luck; only try this exercise when your Maltese is on lead or in a safe area.

Don't expect perfection when teaching these cues to a puppy. Your main goal is to familiarize him and create a positive association with the concepts and the routine.

Once your dog learns the basics, you can start teaching her fun tricks.

BEHAVE!

Your Maltese puppy will begin learning how to behave in your household pack long before he's old enough for formal training. Obviously, housetraining is a major part of this process, but it's not everything. He must learn to relate to everyone in the family: adults, children and other pets. He'll need to learn which behaviors are acceptable and which are not. For instance, teasing a senior dog or trying to steal the cat's food will trigger a very clear message from the recipients of the unwanted attention. Most likely, your Maltese will only try those behaviors once.

Unfortunately, we don't always send our dogs clear and consistent messages. If your puppy is not permitted to play in your flower bed or sleep on your armchair, every member of your family *must* consistently enforce these rules. Oftentimes, that doesn't happen. One person may end up playing the role of strict disciplinarian while another decides to spoil the puppy. If you scold your Maltese when he begs at the table but another family member encourages this behavior, he will become hopelessly confused by these mixed messages. Alternating between praising and reprimanding a dog for the same behavior will drive him crazy.

Therefore, everyone in your household must agree on a care and training schedule before you bring your new Maltese home. Dogs thrive on routines. If you follow a haphazard care regimen when you bring your pup home, it will make his housetraining impossible and undermine his ability to adjust to your home.

START WITH SOCIALIZATION

In a canine pack, puppies begin learning social skills and rules as soon as they become aware of their surroundings. This is an ongoing process of learning and reinforcement that continues until adulthood. Your Maltese puppy may not be ready for formal training, but you should still train and socialize him on a daily basis.

A puppy's critical period for socialization begins around 6 weeks of age and ends around 14 to 16 weeks. During this time, he is mentally attuned to learn and accept new experiences far more easily than as an adult. Make the most of this time by providing your pup with plenty of social interaction and novel experiences.

Although this must include some safety considerations until your dog is fully vaccinated, it's no excuse to wait until he is 4 months old. By then, he will have lost a great deal of his potential. Bringing him along with you on daily errands, visits to friends and short car rides are all wonderful socialization opportunities. Vary the socialization routine and try to intro-

Did You Know?

The key to keeping your Maltese from jumping up inappropriately is consistency. Don't correct your dog for jumping up on you today, and then allow her to do it tomorrow by greeting her with hugs and kisses. As you have learned by now, consistency is critical to all training lessons.

duce him to something or someone new every day. For instance, if you walk him outdoors, vary the surfaces he walks on, such as grass, gravel, concrete or a sandy beach. If you want him to behave sociably around other animals, provide frequent interaction with other species at this age. Most of all, introduce him to a wide array of people: different-looking men, women and children.

After this socialization period ends, your dog may become more reluctant to spontaneously socialize, but it doesn't mean he no longer needs this exposure. Consistently reinforce socialization until he is at least a year old. Don't overwhelm him or push him into experiences if he is clearly fearful, but don't coddle him or neglect his ongoing need for learning and socialization either. This process becomes much simpler after he has completed his shots, when you can finally take him to all the typical dog-friendly places, and you can enroll him in a training or puppy kindergarten program.

In addition to training, classes will help to enhance your Maltese's social skills with other dogs in a safe, controlled setting. Make sure the instructor is experienced in working with toy breeds. Your Maltese will not be able to fully benefit from the class if he feels anxious or threatened by boisterous or aggressive dogs. The instructor should maintain

Turning a shy puppy into a confident adult begins with plenty of proper socialization.

She may be a small puppy now, but without training, your Maltese will grow into a tiny terror in no time.

good control of the environment and ensure that each student receives individual attention as needed.

Continue to reinforce at home the basic obedience training that your pup receives in his weekly classes. Whenever you have a few spare minutes, give your Maltese an impromptu lesson, whether you're teaching him a cue (like sit) or a trick (like speak or shake hands). Your main objective is to learn to communicate with him and instill a positive message about the training process. Always end each session with praise or a treat, regardless of whether your pup has actually learned anything. It will boost his self-confidence and improve his attention span, which is far more important in the long run than achieving instant results. After you've bonded and learned to communicate well with your dog, training will be much easier.

Of course, that doesn't imply that you end up dealing with puppy misbehavior at some point. It's just a normal part of growing up. Chewing, crying and peeing on the rug are simply part of the package when you raise a puppy. Puppies fall prey to housetraining accidents, memory lapses and impulsiveness. Maturity and training will take care of those things.

On the other hand, some types of misbehavior are definitely made worse by the way owners respond to them. For instance, excitedly yelling at a noisy dog to be quiet usually raises the dog's adrenaline level

Oftentimes, a dog's misbehavior is misattributed as separation anxiety. True anxiety results from prior trauma, inadequate early socialization or a chemical imbalance.

When it comes to training, don't baby your baby. Otherwise, she'll never reach her full potential.

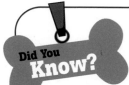

Did You Know? **You can deal with coprophagia — the unpleasant issue of dogs eating their own feces — relatively easily.** Unless your dog has worms, eating feces won't make her sick, but that is no reason to allow her to continue doing it. Some products claim to alleviate the problem, but check with your vet before adding anything to your puppy's diet. Sprinkling hot pepper on the feces is an after-the-fact solution. Prevention is the better way to go: Keep your yard cleaned up.

and encourages louder barking. Constantly scolding a puppy for housetraining accidents will make him reluctant to eliminate in your presence. Instead, he will sneak off to do his business out of your sight. Keep in mind that many dogs chew to relieve stress. Reprimanding a dog for chewing may increase his stress level and lead to him developing other outlets for his anxiety, such as chronically barking or digging.

SEPARATION ANXIETY

"Separation anxiety" is a phrase used to describe a wide range of behavior problems including chronic barking, home destruction or chronic fearfulness. The first step in treating the problem is to ascertain precisely what's going on. As a social species, it is normal for a dog to dislike spending time alone. Even so, most dogs manage to adapt to it. This is not a happenstance occurrence. It requires a combination of training and gradual conditioning to spend time alone.

It is also normal for an unsupervised puppy to indulge in bad habits like barking, house soiling and destructive chewing. Any of these behaviors can be due to boredom, poor supervision or lack of training rather than resulting from a true fear of being alone. Allowing a dog free run of the house to prevent him from barking and

Dogs are pack animals; so, for a happy Maltese, you must assume that role.

Catching your dog in the act of digging is the easiest way to stop the behavior because she will make the "one-plus-one" connection. Too often, though, digging is a solitary occupation — something a lonely dog does out of boredom. Catch your young pup in the act and put a stop to it before you have a yard full of craters.

crying is an unwise trade-off. He will get into trouble, learn bad habits and destroy your home. Make sure your dog is exercised and tired before you leave, and keep him confined to an area where he cannot do damage to your home or to himself while you are gone.

It is possible to train an older puppy or adult Maltese to accept the idea of being alone. Needless to say, it's a complicated and pro-

longed process to correct this behavior. Begin by crating your Maltese for short periods of time or by confining him to a room away from you for long enough to familiarize him with experiencing isolation. At first, this might be just for a few minutes. Reward him for sitting quietly or playing with a toy; don't let him get too excited, which will defeat the purpose.

It's important to avoid overexciting your dog before you leave or when you come home. Keep your arrivals and departures low-key. You might feel guilty about leaving your dog or delighted to see him upon your return. But if he is battling this problem, your exuberance will only make matters worse.

If neither of these approaches helps to dispel the problem, your dog may be suffering from true separation anxiety. Problems on this level can be due to a congenital biochemical imbalance, inadequate socialization as a puppy or severe trauma. For a variety of reasons, the dog's ability to cope with stress has been compromised, leading to physical symptoms ranging from self-mutilation to diarrhea, vomiting or refusal to eat. Seek advice from a veterinarian or behaviorist experienced in dealing with Maltese and separation problems. Some dogs respond well to antianxiety medications or behavior modification. If all else fails, getting another dog to keep him company may be the best solution.

WHINING

It's almost impossible to resist a Maltese puppy, especially one in distress. Puppies

Keep training sessions fun and positive. Reward your Maltese after every session to boost her self-confidence.

instinctively whine if they are cold, hungry or simply want their moms. And a mother is instinctively programmed to come running when she hears the whining. It is perfectly normal for a puppy to continue relying on this system after mak-

ing the transition to a human family because we are no less vulnerable to its effects. The problem is that whining can be triggered by a lot of things that actually don't signify distress. Puppies routinely employ this strategy for any number of things. The desire for a treat, a walk or simply more attention can prompt a bout of whining.

If he fails to get the desired results, your puppy will stop. The problem is that many owners reward whining without even realizing they are doing it. It's an easy trap to fall into. A sad puppy is tough to ignore; it is often easier to comply and quiet him down. Unfortunately, this approach will only lead to longer, louder whining and more demands. If you prefer not to go down this road, you first need to train yourself to stop responding to it. Whenever your puppy commences unwanted whining, tell him to be quiet and don't give into his demands.

Dogs love to chew things, edible or not. If you want to keep yours out of your goodies, give her a proper chew toy instead.

CHEWING

Chewing is a perfectly normal — and even healthy — canine pastime. Dogs do it because they enjoy it. In some ways, it's a good thing. It can keep a dog occupied for hours and helps to clean his teeth.

Maltese aren't known for major destructive chewing, but don't make the mistake of thinking of it as a temporary habit your puppy will outgrow. Instead, train your Maltese to direct his chewing appropriately. Make sure he has appealing chew toys available. Keep potentially tasty valuables out of your pup's reach, and keep your eyes on him. As your puppy matures, he will become less likely to chew inappropriate items. A puppy, however, can't be expected to have good judgment or a reliable memory regarding these things.

Your Maltese wants to make you happy. Make sure she's paying attention during training sessions, and your repetition and positive reinforcement will be successful.

If your pup becomes possessive of her food, look for other signs of future aggression, such as guarding her favorite toys or refusing to follow obedience cues that she knows. Consult an obedience trainer for help in reinforcing obedience so your Maltese will fully understand that you are the boss.

As long as you train your Maltese to direct his chewing appropriately, it can be a great way to keep him occupied. Appropriate chewing will also help keep his teeth in good condition. Inappropriate chewing will not only result in damage to your home, but it can also lead to broken teeth or worse.

When you discover your Maltese happily chomping on a forbidden item, tell him "no" and remove the object, then redirect him to one of his toys. You'll probably have to repeat this lesson frequently before your message sinks in. Chewing deterrents such as Grannik's Bitter Apple®, oil or cloves sometimes help discourage a puppy from chewing, but they're not always completely effective. Good supervision is the only reliable deterrent.

NIPPING

Maltese don't typically grow up to be nippers or growlers. These behaviors are a result of poor training; they're much more easily prevented than cured.

Puppies learn their first lessons in bite control from their mothers, which is another important reason why they should remain with her for a few extra weeks. She won't hesitate to scold them for playing too rough or for nipping her.

After your puppy transitions to life with humans, you'll need to continue these socialization lessons. In some cases, this idea needs a lot of reinforcement. Spend at least 15 minutes a day playing with your puppy, especially if nipping has already started to become a problem.

A puppy can easily get carried away while he plays, and he might not even be aware of what he is doing. It is your job to remind him that nipping peoples' hands is not acceptable. If his teeth touch your skin (whether or not it actually hurts), tell him "no" and immediately halt the play session until he calms down. Ignoring this behavior while he is young can set the stage for habits that are much more difficult to revise when he is older.

Excessive Barking

Barking is a self-rewarding behavior. It will take something far more attractive or very aversive to stop a dog from excessively barking. Yelling at her to be quiet just adds to the fun; to your dog, it just means you've joined in the bark fest.

You can reprogram some dogs to quit the annoying behavior through various positive reinforcement-shaping techniques, but others get so much joy out of barking that they won't care what treats, toys or activities you use as bait.

There are other dogs that will be quiet while you are around but will sound off when you're not home. Most likely, these dogs are territorial barkers. They feel an instinctive duty to keep "strangers" at bay, even if the strangers are squirrels or sparrows. To such a dog, an intruder is a trespasser, no matter the size or species.

Some dogs bark because of separation anxiety. You may suspect that your dog has this disorder if she's quiet and relaxed when you're home, but you get reports from exasperated neighbors that she has spent the entire day barking at nothing. This type of barking is probably the most difficult to cure. The more the dog is punished for the behavior, the worse it becomes, but this doesn't mean it can't be cured. Using homeopathic treatments and behavior-modification tactics usually work.

It may take some time to cure the excessive barking. To do so using positive reinforcement, you'll need to be consistent and dedicated. If you're using food as a reward, it's best to use your puppy's regular kibble; otherwise, you'll fill her up with treats and she won't want to eat her normal meals.

Before you begin, arm yourself with a pouch or bag to carry her food, a supply of kibble, a squeak toy and a clicker. The squeaker will act as a distracter, the clicker will reinforce the appropriate behavior and the kibble will reward the appropriate behavior.

Put your puppy in a situation where she normally would bark. Praise, click and reward while she's quiet. If she barks, use the squeaker until she stops to investigate. When she does so, praise, click and reward again. Repeat throughout the training session.

Each time you put your puppy in a situation where she will bark, have your tools close at hand. Use them consistently and be patient. It will take some time for her to overcome a self-rewarding behavior such as barking.

STARS OF

THE SHOW

A glamorous little extrovert like the Maltese seems like a natural for the show ring. He is a perpetual standout in the conformation ring, often described as one of the "glamour breeds." His versatility, athleticism and intelligence also give him an impressive edge when in performance competition.

The Maltese is suited for many areas of dog sports, but there is a lot more to success than simply picking the right breed. Winning is the obvious reward, but that should never be your sole reason for choosing this hobby. Dog sports were designed as an objective means of evaluating various canine qualities. These range from physical structure and breed-specific traits that are evaluated in the conformation ring to obedience and agility competitions that test a dog's mental skills and dexterity. Events like tracking measure a dog's aptitude and instinct. What they all have in common is that lots of time and effort go into the finished product. Stepping into the ring with your Maltese to give a show-stopping performance is merely the last step in a long, arduous process.

In any type of competition, the handler's job is to become invisible. You are there to enhance your dog's performance, but this contribution must seem effortless and unnoticed. On the surface, those may seem like contradictory objectives. The thing that makes it possible is the bond and communication between dog and handler. Points and titles are satisfying, but these qualities are ultimately the biggest rewards to be gained from competitive dog sports. Nothing can compare to the satisfaction of perfectly synchronized teamwork with your dog.

SMART TIP!

Don't rush to compete. At physical maturity, Maltese often still need time to mature mentally. Maltese live for a long time and are basically healthy dogs, which allows them to compete long after many larger dogs must retire.

EVALUATING YOUR SHOW PROSPECT

It's often said that the average exhibitor has a five-year tenure in dog sports. That's because most novices are unprepared for the challenges and commitment needed to be successful. You must be prepared to take some knocks when first starting out. Some will be justified; some will not. Either way, it's much easier to cope with them if you have confidence in the dog you're showing.

The first step to success is choosing a good show prospect. This is easier said than done. Almost every successful exhibitor started off with the wrong dog. He may have been a bit too large or small, or maybe he didn't have the stamina or temperament for the show ring. Most often, these dogs were not chosen with performance in mind. If you are serious about showing, it should be a primary factor when selecting your Maltese, not something to be considered after the fact. You may feel that your Maltese is the most intelligent and beautiful dog in the world, but that doesn't necessarily mean the show world will agree. It can lead to disappointment if you try to put a square peg in a round hole.

If you are hoping to purchase a Maltese for show, make this clear to the breeder in advance. Producing competitive dogs is the goal of any serious breeding program. Experienced breeders regularly compete their own dogs in one or more dog sports. They are well-acquainted with the qualities that make a winning Maltese, and they do not want their name represented in the show ring by dogs that don't belong there.

A show-potential puppy will adhere to the description outlined in the breed standard. He should be an exceptional specimen. This doesn't just include breed-specific traits like proportion, expression and proper coat. He must also possess robust health, mental and physical stamina and sturdy structure. Physical soundness must be equaled by mental soundness. These qualities are even more important for Maltese competing in performance events. A beautiful coat may hide a weak front or topline, but these physical shortcomings will seriously undermine his athletic ability.

Stability is especially important for toy breeds. The last thing you need is for your Maltese to "run out of gas" because stress has undermined his appetite. The ability to cope with all kinds of stress is essential for any show dog.

CONFORMATION

Watching a dog show on TV, or even ringside, can give a false impression of what is really going on. Judging may seem like an arbitrary process, resulting in unexplainable capricious choices, and handling may seem no more challenging than taking your dog for a walk. However, there is a lot more to it than that.

The evaluation process of conformation shows involves comparing each dog to the description in its official breed standard. The standard is actually a "standard of perfection," and no dog in existence can match it. Dogs are gradually eliminated from competition based on how well they conform to this description. This process of elimination

Conformation events are a great way to show off your dog.

is employed at all shows, even when different breeds compete against each other. There are three types of conformation dog shows, involving different amounts of competition against other breeds.

Specialty shows are open to only one breed. They usually attract very large entries of top-quality Maltese from all over the country. But the fact that specialty shows tend to attract much larger numbers of entries in a particular breed makes them much more competitive. Simply winning a class placement at a large specialty show can be a thrilling achievement.

Group shows are limited to the breeds in a specific AKC group, such as the Toy Group. The best representative of each toy breed will compete for first, second, third and fourth place. All breed shows are open to every recognized breed. Maltese first compete against members of their own breed for Best of Breed. The winner moves to the next stage of competition against all the other toy breeds. After defeating the other Best of Breed winners in his respective group, he enters the final phase of the elimination process. Best In Show competition is limited to seven group winners. From these, one dog is ultimately selected as the winner.

Every dog in the show is entered in one of several classes offered for that particular breed, such as puppy, novice, bred by exhibitor and open. These classes are divided by sex, and males are judged first. The judge will examine each dog individually. The handler then walks the dog to demonstrate its soundness and demeanor. The winners of each male (dog) class return to the ring to compete against one another for Winners Dog. One dog is selected as winner and runner up as reserve winner. The whole process is then repeated for the female (bitch) classes.

One to five championship points are awarded each win depending on geographic region and the number of dogs defeated in competition. To become an AKC champion, a dog must accumulate 15 points, including two wins worth at least 3 points each.

After Winners Dog and Winners Bitch are selected, both return to the ring to compete against the champions for Best of Breed and Best of Opposite Sex to Best of Breed and Best of Winners. Nonchampion dogs can, and often do, defeat the champions during this phase of the judging.

Children of any age can show dogs in regular conformation classes. There is no age limit, but participating in Junior Showmanship allows them to compete against their peers while perfecting their

If you aren't into competitive dog sports, be sure to find other ways to keep your Maltese active.

Musical Freestyle

Musical canine freestyle, or "dancing with dogs," is a sport that began in Canada around 1990 and is now swinging into popularity around the world. Heelwork and agility-type exercises are choreographed to the handler's choice of music. The dog heels left and right, circles, spins, walks backward, walk sideways or weaves through her handler's legs. The music keeps dog and handler focused together and makes the experience enjoyable for performers and spectators alike.

Freestyle is one of the most fun ways to improve a dog's concentration and attention to signals. It is also a wonderful exercise for both dog and handler. The greatest benefit of this sport, however, is the bond that deepens between the dance partners.

To start teaching your Maltese to do freestyle, first teach her to focus her attention on your voice, face and hands. A treat or a toy lure that your dog can hone in on will help. At first, put on some music that makes you want to tap your toes and makes your Maltese want to practice heeling with attention and happy prancing. Medium-speed music with a definable beat is good to start with. The music should enhance what you're doing and make you feel good. Your Maltese will respond naturally to your upbeat mood.

Step to the rhythm, but you don't necessarily have to hit every beat. Just walk smoothly and let the music suggest movements to you. Do big circles, left and right, then work to smaller circles. If you've done any obedience work, you might try figure-eights, recalls, swing finishes and send outs.

If your dog knows some tricks, go ahead and incorporate them into your freestyle routine. Tricks make for some unique performances.

presentation skills. It provides an opportunity for a child to develop confidence and ability before venturing into the conformation ring. Many highly successful professional handlers began their careers in Junior Showmanship.

Rather than judging the dogs, the handlers are evaluated on professionalism, skill and ability to follow judges' instructions. However an eye-catching, well-trained dog will certainly improve the chances of winning. Junior Showmanship is open to children age 10 to 18. Classes are divided into Novice and Open divisions by age. Competitors that have already won three first prizes must compete in Open class.

TRAINING FOR COMPETITION

Stress management is partly genetic and partly learned. The genetic aspect should figure prominently in your selection criteria for a show puppy. Part of raising a show prospect is conditioning to maximize this. Serious exhibitors begin training and socializing their puppies from a very young age. They are thoroughly familiarized with the equipment, the routine and the environment of their future career. In addition to that, a puppy destined for a competitive career must be comfortable with things like traveling, eating and sleeping in a crate, adjusting to weather changes, receiving attention from strangers and

accepting variations in his normal routine. It is difficult and sometimes impossible, to begin introducing an adult dog to enjoy these things

If you have a show-prospect Maltese, start training him to stand for examination and walk on a lead as soon as you get him. Once he has completed his puppy vaccinations, he should attend a training class. This will get him accustomed to the varied atmosphere of a dog show and teach him to focus and concentrate despite distractions. Specialized instruction for obedience, agility or conformation competitions are also essential but may not be advisable until he is a little older. Serious competitors attend a lot of classes to keep their dogs in top form.

Daily routine training at home is equally important. You should also arrange occasional outings to dog shows into your Maltese's training, even though he may not be old enough to compete. But don't subject him to formal competition until he is ready. A good show prospect can be ruined by pushing him too hard or too fast.

Match shows are a great way to prepare your dog for the demands of competition. For one thing, match shows offer classes for puppies younger than 6 months old. They must be at least 6 months old to enter a real dog show. Aspiring, underage show dogs, novice handlers and judges can all hone their skills this way.

Don't underestimate how important these practice runs can be. No matter how well you perform at home or at class, competition at a public venue is a whole different story. Even professional handlers admit to suffering preshow jitters. This can ruin the most practiced performance. Unlike some other breeds, preparing a Maltese for show is complicated. Plenty of practice is the best way to devise a fool-proof routine.

OBEDIENCE

Obedience first became a formal competitive event at AKC shows in 1936. Demonstrations by highly trained dogs had been consistently popular at shows for decades prior to that. But there had been no program to objectively evaluate the dogs' skills or award official titles. Unlike in conformation competitions, obedience dogs are assessed solely on their performance skills. Neutered dogs and those with undocumented backgrounds and disqualifying faults can still compete in obedience.

But don't assume that obedience is for dogs that cannot cut it in conformation. This branch of the sport is often regarded as the most stressful, exacting and demanding for handlers as well as dogs. A dog's mental and physical fitness is subjected to quite a test. Although his appearance isn't included in the evaluation, obedience dogs are still on public display.

The competition involves a combination of group and individual exercises that dogs and handlers perform at a judge's direction. Obedience trials are offered at specialty and all-breed shows, and competition is open to all registered dogs older than 6 months old.

Judging is conducted as a process of elimination. Rather than comparing each dog to a description in a standard, the judge evaluates each dog against his mental picture of an ideal performance for each exercise.

Each dog/handler team begins with 200 points, and judges deduct for errors in each exercise. To earn a title, a dog must earn at least half the points allotted for each exercise, with a minimum overall total of 170 points. Qualifying dogs are awarded a green

Regular agility equipment might be too large for your small dog. The Teacup Dogs Agility Association is a great alternative.

ribbon and first through fourth placements are awarded in each regular class.

There are three levels of competition. Novice, Open and Utility are made up of gradually more complex routines for dogs of increasing levels of skill. There are also six noncompetitive classes that dogs can enter: prenovice, graduate novice, graduate open, brace, veteran and versatility.

At the Novice level, dogs compete for a Companion Dog title. They must qualify with scores of 170 at three different shows. Novice dog competition includes six basic exercises:

◆ heel on lead and figure eight
◆ stand for examination
◆ heel free
◆ recall
◆ long sit (one minute)
◆ long down (three minutes)

Open competition is made up of seven exercises. They include more off-lead work, jumping and retrieving. Handlers can direct their dogs during the competition using either vocal or hand signals. But some exercises must be completed without the handler in the dog's presence. Dogs earning three qualifying scores at this level are awarded the Companion Dog Excellent title. The seven basic exercises are:

◆ heel off lead and figure eight
◆ drop on recall
◆ retrieve on the flat

◆ retrieve over a high jump
◆ broad jump
◆ long sit (three minutes with handler out of sight)
◆ long down (five minutes with handler out of sight)

Utility Dog is the highest level of obedience competition. These exercises are designed to test a dog's ability to discriminate scents and respond to hand signals. Handlers are not permitted to use vocal commands during these exercises. There are six exercises at this level:

◆ signal exercise
◆ scent discrimination article 1
◆ scent discrimination article 2
◆ directed retrieve
◆ stand and examination
◆ directed jump

RALLY OBEDIENCE

Rally was added to AKC's roster of companion events in 2005. Since then, it has become one of the most popular with competitors and spectators alike. It was originally intended as an introductory step for beginning obedience competitors, but it has gained status as a competitive event in its own right.

Dog–handler teams navigate the rally course at their own pace, and handlers are allowed to encourage their dogs, which is

---

Canine competitions, like obedience and rally events, are great ways to keep an active Maltese entertained.

not permitted in obedience. Teamwork and communication are evaluated, along with skill and precision.

The rally course consists of 10 to 20 "stations" (designated stops where the handler directs the dog to perform a specific exercise). Each dog/handler team begins with 100 points, and points are deducted for errors. To earn a title, the dog must earn three qualifying scores of 70 or better from two different judges.

In 2005, the AKC began offering three levels of awards in rally obedience: novice, advanced and excellent. The novice level consists of 10 to 15 exercises performed on lead. Handlers are permitted to encourage their dogs with praise and gestures. Dogs earn a Rally Novice title after earning three qualifying scores.

The rally advanced course consists of 12 to 17 stations. All exercises must be completed off lead. There are two divisions, A and B, based on prior titles and experience. Dogs earning three qualifying scores in Rally Advanced earn the RA title.

In rally excellent competition, 15 to 20 stations must be completed off lead. Verbal encouragements are permitted, but hand signals aren't. Like rally advanced, A and B divisions are offered. Dogs that earn three qualifying scores attain a Rally Excellent title.

Titled dogs may also compete for Advanced Excellent titles by qualifying in both Advanced B and Excellent B classes at 10 different trials.

AGILITY

Agility is another challenging sport perfect for agile, energetic athletic dogs. The mental and physical challenges posed by different exercises and unpredictable obstacle courses often appeal to dogs that don't care for the regimented nature of obedience.

The sport debuted in England in 1978 and became an official AKC event in 1994. It is tremendously popular with exhibitors of small breeds. Their quick reflexes and natural dexterity gave them a definite advantage.

The concept is roughly modeled on equestrian show jumping. The agility course can be likened to a canine playground. The course will vary, but each entrant receives a map showing the route and obstacles and each gets an advance "walk through" to familiarize them with the details of the course. The basic course includes 16 to 20 obstacles. These will include a mixture of tables, tunnels, chutes, hurdles, A-frames, and weave poles. At advanced levels, these courses become more complex with things like bridges and contact obstacles that dogs must touch with a paw while running the course. Handlers are permitted to provide encouragements, praise and signals for their dogs during competition.

Certain features of the course, such as the height of hurdles, are modified for smaller dogs. Competitions are divided into five size divisions and three levels: Novice, Open, and Agility Excellent.

To earn an agility title, dogs are required to earn three scores within the time and fault limit. A qualifying score is a minimum of 85 out of a possible 100 points.

If you want to try agility with your Maltese, make sure he's fit enough for the demands of running and jumping. If your vet gives the OK, enroll your dog in an agility training class. Agility seminars, workshops and classes are offered through many dog-training clubs. It's a good idea to start with these for practice before entering an agility trial. This will give you needed training and a chance to prepare for the physical challenges.

TRACKING

Tracking is open to all recognized breeds. Dogs are evaluated solely on their natural ability to find and follow a scent trail. Every dog has some aptitude for this work, but you can encourage it by enrolling your Maltese in a tracking club. Before entering, your Maltese in an official tracking dog test, he must be certified as eligible. The certifying judge will provide you with certification forms allowing you to enter your Maltese in four tracking tests within a one-year period. Each dog must wear a harness and a 20 to 40 foot lead during the test. Tests aren't timed, but it's up to the judge to determine if the dog's actually following a trail or if he's lost the track.

To earn a Tracking Dog title, the dog is required to follow a scent trail approximately 500 yards over an open field to locate a glove or wallet. This scent trail is laid out 30 minutes to two hours prior to testing, including three to five turns.

For Tracking Dog Excellent, the requirements become more challenging. The trail is 800 to 1,000 yards long, three to five hours old with five to seven turns and various obstacles like roads, ditches and diversionary tracks. The dog must locate four different items in this test.

The highest level, Variable Surface Tracking, tests the dog's ability to follow a scent trail 3 to 5 hours old over different terrains. This trail ranges from 600 to 800 yards in length, with four to eight turns. The dog must locate four different items in this test.

A dog earning all three titles becomes a Champion Tracker.

Since 2001, the AKC has offered a Versatility Companion title for dogs competing successfully in obedience, agility and tracking. Dogs can earn four levels of titles from VCD 1 to VCD 4.

NOTABLE & QUOTABLE

Maltese thrive on the physical and mental stimulation agility offers. Agility creates an opportunity to develop a special bond between you and your companion that no other dog sport can offer. I highly recommend it!

— Brenda Morris, a Maltese breeder and trainer based in Las Vegas, Nev.

Smart owners can find out more information about this popular and fascinating breed by contacting the organizations listed below. They will be glad to help you dig deeper into the world of the Maltese, and you won't even have to beg!

Academy of Veterinary Homeopathy: Founded in 1995, the AVH is comprised of vets who share the common desire to restore their patients' true health using homeopathic treatments. www.theavh.org

American Animal Hospital Association: The AAHA accredits small-animal hospitals throughout the United States and Canada. www.healthypet.com

American Dog Owners Association: The ADOA is the nation's oldest and largest member-based organization representing dog owners for responsible dog ownership. www.adoa.org

American Holistic Veterinary Medical Association: This association explores and supports alternative and complementary approaches to veterinary healthcare and is dedicated to integrating all aspects of animal wellness in a socially and environmentally responsible manner. www.ahvma.org

The American Kennel Club was established in 1884. It is America's oldest kennel club. **The United Kennel Club is the second oldest in the United States.** It began registering dogs in 1898.

it's a
Fact

American Humane Association: Founded in 1877, the AHA is a nonprofit membership organization dedicated to protecting children and animals. www.americanhumane.org

American Kennel Club Canine Health Foundation: This foundation is largest non-profit funder of exclusively canine research in the world. www.akcchf.org

American Kennel Club: The AKC website offers information and links to conformation, tracking, rally, obedience and agility programs, member clubs and all things dog. www.akc.org

American Maltese Association: The national club's website includes breeder listings and more. www.americanmaltese.org

American Society for the Prevention of Cruelty to Animals: The ASPCA was the first humane organization in the Western Hemisphere. Its mission is "to provide effective means for the prevention of cruelty to animals throughout the United States." www.aspca.org

American Veterinary Medical Association: This nonprofit represents more than 80,000 vets working in private and corporate practice, government, industry, academia and uniformed services.www.avma.org

Association of American Feed Control Officials: The AAFCO develops and implements uniform and equitable laws, regulations, standards and enforcement policies for regulating the manufacturing, distribution and sale of animal feeds, which results in the production of safe, effective and useful feeds. www.aafco.org

Association of Pet Dog Trainers: A professional organization of individual dog trainers committed to becoming better trainers through education. www.apdt.com

Canadian Kennel Club: Our northern neighbor's oldest kennel club is similar to the AKC in this country. www.ckc.ca

Canine Performance Events: Sports help keep dogs active. www.k9cpe.com

Delta Society: This organization offers animal assistance to people in need. www.deltasociety.org

Dog Scouts of America: Take your dog to camp. www.dogscouts.com

Fédération Cynologique Internationale: The World Canine Organization includes 84 members and contract partners (one member per country), all who issue their own pedigrees and train their own judges. www.fci.be

Love on a Leash: This is a therapy dog organization. Your sweet dog has a lot of love to give others. www.loveonaleash.org

National Association of Professional Pet Sitters: When you'll be away for a while, hire someone to watch and entertain your dog. www.petsitters.org

North American Dog Agility Council: This site provides links to clubs, obedience trainers and agility trainers in the United States and Canada. www.nadac.com

Pet Care Services Association: This nonprofit trade association includes nearly 3,000 pet-care service businesses in the United States and around the world. www.petcareservices.org

Pet Sitters International: This organization's mission is to educate professional pet sitters and to promote, support and recognize excellence in pet sitting. www.petsit.com

Teacup Dogs Agility Association: The Maltese certainly fits this association's purpose: to provide a competitive venue for dogs of small stature without regard to the dogs' breed or pedigree. www.teacupagility.com

Therapy Dogs Inc.: Get your Maltese involved in therapy work. www.therapydogs.com

Therapy Dogs International: Find more therapy dog info here: www.tdi-dog.org

United Kennel Club: The UKC offers several of the events offered by the AKC, including agility, conformation and obedience. In addition, the UKC offers competitions in hunting and dog sport (companion and protective events). www.ukcdogs.com

United States Dog Agility Association: The USDAA has info on training, clubs and events in the United States, Canada, Mexico and overseas. www.usdaa.com

World Canine Freestyle Organization: This association organizes competitions in the fun new sport of dog dancing. www. worldcaninefreestyle.org

SMART TIP! **Remember to keep your dog's leash slack when interacting with other dogs.** It is not unusual for a dog to pick out one or two canine neighbors to dislike. If you know there's bad blood, step off to the side and put a barrier, such as a parked car, between the dogs. If there are no barriers nearby, move to the side of the walkway, then cue your dog to sit, stay and watch you until his nemesis passes. Then continue your walk.

DOGGIE DAY CARE

Any day-care program can also be a great place for your Maltese to play and socialize.

It can be the best exercise option for this breed during inclement weather. Maltese are weather-sensitive, and walking a little white dog in wet, dirty weather is no fun. Even moderately sized day-care facilities offer ample space for a Maltese workout.

Before your dog is accepted into a day-care program, you may be asked to provide proof of vaccination or health certification from your vet. You may also be asked to bring your pup for an introductory interview to assess his personality. Day care can be very beneficial for dogs in need of a little extra social bonding, but it is not recommended for dogs with major behavior problems such as severe shyness or aggression.

Keep these points in mind when choosing a day-care program:

● Do the staff members provide good supervision and positive interaction with the dogs?

● Are they familiar with small breeds' health and safety requirements?

● Is emergency medical treatment easily accessible?

● Are the dogs maintained in manageable groups that get along well with one another? (Large and small dogs should never be enclosed together.)

● Does the facility look and smell clean?

● Is it securely enclosed? This should include double gates and doors at all entrances, as well as secure fencing for very small dogs.

DOG WALKERS

A professional dog walker is another helpful addition to routine dog care. Like day care, a dog walker can contribute to your dog's social life and help fill the hours while you are at work.

For an owner who works full time, a dog walker can be indispensable. The walker's daily visits reinforce a consistent house-training schedule and help prevent accidents. It also provides social interaction and helps a dog adjust to spending time alone. Often, dogs look forward to the daily visits and learn to cope in their owners'

Take your Maltese to a dog park specially designed with small dogs in mind. Toy breeds can squeeze through fencing easily or get trampled by larger dogs.

absence, which enhances the pup's confidence and offsets any tendencies toward separation anxiety.

Professional dog walkers can range from full-time professionals to school-age children. In order to select the right person for your Maltese, you'll need to consider a few different factors.

Be sure to check for the person's references and background information before entrusting anyone with your house keys or your pet. Make sure the person is reliable enough to arrive at the same time every day. Otherwise, the service will be useless

in reinforcing a daily schedule. You may want to accompany the person on a walk to reassure yourself and your dog. Make sure that your dog feels comfortable with the walker and that the person has experience interacting with toy breeds. This is especially important if the person customarily walks dogs in groups or takes them to dog parks.

DOG PARKS

Although he needs outdoor exercise, public places can expose your Maltese to many potential dangers; so be vigilant.

Did You Know?

Some communities have created regular dog runs and separate spaces for small dogs. These small-dog runs are ideal for introducing puppies to the dog-park experience. The runs are smaller, the participants are smaller and their owners are often more vigilant because they are used to watching out for their fragile companions.

Did You Know?

The dog run is one of the few urban spaces where a dog can be off leash. To enter most dog parks, dogs must be fully vaccinated and healthy, and females must not be in heat.

Bicycles, baby strollers, large dogs and pedestrians can all do serious damage to a tiny dog. Maltese should never be allowed to play off-lead in places where large dogs can access them.

One way to minimize dangerous sidewalk encounters is to exercise your Maltese in a dog park. In recent years, dog parks have become staples of almost every major city, providing a solution to limited exercise areas for pets. They offer a safe, secure and dog friendly environment for pets and owners to exercise and socialize. You will quickly discover that your Maltese is irresistible to strangers. Expect to make a lot of friends and answer plenty of questions every time you take him for an outing.

You may be able to locate dog parks in your city through an internet search. Or try asking your dog-walking neighbors, vets, dog groomers or trainers about canine recreation areas in your area.

Once you've located some dog parks, check them out alone before bringing your Maltese along. Some dog parks are open to the public but may restrict play areas to large or small breeds. Others are private, and access is restricted to members.

All the parks have rules to ensure safety and hygiene. Most require that dogs be fully vaccinated and wear ID, rabies and license tags. Some do not allow puppies under six months old, females in season, aggressive dogs or owners bringing more than three dogs at one time. Owners are required to clean up after their dogs and supervise them adequately to prevent fighting or overly rough play.

The basic rules usually vary to some extent, and every dog park has its own individual atmosphere depending on the type of dogs and owners who frequent it. The mood at the park will have the greatest affect on whether or not your dog feels comfortable there. Maintaining and sharing a dog park necessitates courtesy and cooperation.

Look for these things when choosing a dog park for your toy breed:

Security: Fencing should be high enough to prevent big dogs from jumping over or small ones from squeezing under. Double gates will help avert escapes. Some parks provide segregated play areas for large and small dogs. Each area should be clearly designated and fenced.

Sanitation: Clean-up tools, disinfectant, plastic bags and receptacles should be available. All hard surfaces should be disinfected regularly. Depending on the amount of dog traffic, this might be daily or weekly.

Safety: The park should be accessible to emergency services. If there is seating for humans, dogs will inevitably jump and climb on it. It must be sturdy with, slats closely spaced to prevent any dog's leg or paw from getting caught. If the park has no trees, a shaded area should be provided. Some dog parks have onsite water supplies; some don't. But water should always be available.

CAR TRAVEL

Familiarize your Maltese with riding in your car at an early age. You may or may not take him in the car often, but he'll at least need to go to the vet. And you don't want these trips to be traumatic for your dog or troublesome for you. The safest way for a dog to ride in a car is in his crate. If he uses a crate in the house, you can use the same one for travel.

Another option is a specially made safety harness for dogs, which will straps your Maltese in the car similar to how a seat belt secures you. Do not let your dog roam loose in the vehicle; it's really dangerous! If you have to break quickly, your dog can get thrown and injured. If your dog starts climbing on you and pestering you while you're driving, you won't be able to concentrate on the road. It is an unsafe situation for everyone — human and canine.

On long car rides, stop often to let your dog relieve himself. Bring along whatever you need to clean up after him, including some paper towels and perhaps some old bath towels to use if he has an accident in the car or suffers from motion sickness.

IDENTIFICATION

Your Maltese is your valued companion and friend. That is why you always keep a close eye on him, and you have made sure that he can't escape from the yard or wriggle out of his collar and run away from you. However, accidents can happen, and there may come a time when your dog unexpectedly gets separated from you. If this happens, the first thing on your mind will be finding him. Proper identification — including an ID tag, a tattoo and possibly a microchip — will increase the chances of him returning to you safely and quickly.

An ID tag on a collar or harness is the primary means of pet identification (and ID licenses are required in many communities, anyway). Although they're inexpensive and easy to read, collars and ID tags can come off or be removed.

A microchip won't get lost. Containing a unique ID number that can be read by scanners, the microchip is embedded underneath a dog's skin. It's invaluable for identifying lost or stolen pets. However, to be effective, the microchip must be registered in a national database, and smart owners should make sure their contact info is kept up-to-date. Not every shelter or veterinary clinic has a scanner; nor do most people who might pick up and try to return a lost pet. So your best bet is to get both!

INDEX

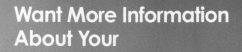
MALTESE, a Smart Owner's Guide™

part of the Kennel Club Books® Interactive Series™

LIBRARY OF CONGRESS CATALOGING-IN-PUBLICATION DATA

Fernandez, Amy.
  Maltese / [Amy Fernandez].
      p. cm. — (A smart owner's guide)
  Includes bibliographical references and index.
  ISBN 978-1-59378-750-9
  1. Maltese dog. I. Title.
  SF429.M25F374 2011
  636.76—dc22

                    2010031587

JOIN
**Club
Maltese™**
TODAY!